100
THINGS TO DO IN
HOLLAND, MI
BEFORE YOU
DIE

Tiptoe through the tulips at Nelis' Dutch Village.

100

THINGS TO DO IN
HOLLAND, MI
BEFORE YOU
DIE

VERONICA BAREMAN

Library of Congress Control Number: 2023935483

ISBN: 9781681064628

Design by Jill Halpin

Photos by author unless otherwise noted.

Printed in the United States of America
23 24 25 26 27   5 4 3 2 1

DEDICATION

Thank you, God, for so many answered prayers. For Dan, who is my biggest supporter, encourager, and cheerleader, no matter what wild and crazy adventure upon which I embark. Life would not be so sweet without you along on this journey.

The DeZwaan Windmill
of Windmill Island Gardens

CONTENTS

Preface. xiii

Acknowledgments. xiv

Food and Drink

  1. Taste Blueberry-Flavored Everything at Bowerman's Blueberries . . .2

  2. Call in Your Order at Russ' Restaurant 4

  3. Learn the Secrets of Holland with Holland Tasting Tours 6

  4. Take a Break from Your Inner Dutch at the Curragh Irish Pub. 7

  5. Taste a Tommy Turtle at Captain Sundae 8

  6. Listen for the Whinny at Crazy Horse Steakhouse. 9

  7. Indulge in a Bacon-Flavored Donut at DeBoer Bakkerij
     and Dutch Brothers Restaurant **10**

  8. Get a Taste of the Old Country at the Wooden Shoe Restaurant 12

  9. Create a Masterpiece in a Bowl at Peachwave. **14**

10. Say Hello to Fresh Food and Friendly Service
    at Waverly Stone Gastropub. **15**

11. Chug a Local Favorite at New Holland Brewing Company. **16**

12. Bite into an MGB Burger at Goog's Pub & Grub **17**

13. Belly Up to a Delicious Brew at the 205 Coffee Bar. **18**

14. Practice Your Pronunciation at Lemonjello's **20**

15. Tickle Your Tongue with a Premium-Crafted Spirit
    at Coppercraft Distillery **22**

16. Feed Your Need for Hashbrowns at Windmill Restaurant. **23**

• •

17. Stroll through Washington Square and Discover
the Biscuit Café **24**

18. Get Your Fill of Fish at Boatwerks Waterfront Restaurant **25**

19. Taste the Finer Things in Life at Butch's Dry Dock **26**

20. Get Some Down-Home Comfort Pizza **27**

21. Enjoy a Historic Taste of Italiano at Fricano's Too **28**

22. Sip a Cider and Taste a Pie at Crane's in the City **29**

23. Taste Authentic Mexican Flavor at Margarita's
Mexican Restaurant **30**

Music and Entertainment

24. Pack a Picnic and Practice Your Dance Moves at Kollen Park's
Summer Concert Series **34**

25. Soak Up the Local Talent at Holland Community Theatre **35**

26. Thrill Your Inner Thespian at Hope College
Repertory Theatre **36**

27. Feel the History of Holland at Park Theater **38**

28. Increase Artistic Awareness at Knickerbocker Theatre **39**

29. Feel the Freedom at the Independence Day
Fireworks Celebration **40**

30. Attend an Event at Holland Civic Center Place **42**

31. Kick Your Feet Up at Sperry's Moviehouse **44**

32. Party Hearty at the Annual LAUP Fiesta **46**

33. Get Educated about Agriculture at the Ottawa County Fair **47**

34. Take In the Local Talent with the Summer Street
Performer Series **48**

• •

35. Step into the Future at Zero Latency Holland **50**

36. Celebrate a World of Music at the International Festival
of Holland **51**

37. Expand Your Mind and Your Digital Experience at Herrick
District Library **52**

38. Let the Music Take You Away at Holland Symphony Orchestra . . .**53**

Sports and Recreation

39. Pet a Pig or a Pony at Fellinlove Farm. **56**

40. Spend a Day on the Lake with Holland Water Sports **57**

41. Walk through a Dune at Tunnel Park. **58**

42. Give Your Pedometer a Workout at Holland State Park Pier. **59**

43. Say Goodnight to the Sun at Holland State Park Beach **60**

44. Get the Best View of Lake Michigan on Mt. Pisgah **61**

45. Strap on a Pair of Ice Skates at Griff's Icehouse West. **62**

46. Paddle Your Heart Out with Tulip City Paddle Tours **63**

47. Nurture Nature at Degraaf Nature Center **64**

48. Discover the Outdoors at the Outdoor Discovery Center **65**

49. Listen for the Pew Pew of Laser Fire at the Lost City **66**

50. Embrace Your Inner Child at BAM! Entertainment Center **67**

51. Cheer On the Home Team with a Hope College Athletics Event . . .**68**

52. Catch Tonight's Dinner with a Sport Fishing Charter **70**

53. Have a Hands-On Sailing Experience with Deep Lake Ventures
Sailboat Charters **72**

54. Make a Splash at the Holland Aquatic Center. **74**

● ●

55. Fall Asleep to the Sound of Crashing Waves in an Unsalted Vacations Rental **75**

56. Shoosh through Blankets of Snow at Pigeon Creek Park **76**

57. Rent an E-Bike at Velo City Cycles. **78**

58. Lower Your Blood Pressure at Window on the Waterfront **80**

59. Ogle the Outdoors on Holland's Nature Trails **81**

Culture and History

60. Sleep above the Action on 8th Street at Teerman Lofts. **84**

61. Surround Yourself with Artistry at the Holland Area Arts Council. . .**85**

62. Find Your Inner Artist by Painting and Hiding Rocks. **86**

63. Follow the Yellow Brick Road to the Holland Oz Exhibit **87**

64. Take a Walk down Memory Lane at the Holland Museum **88**

65. Stand in the Shoes of Holland's Early Residents at the Cappon House & Settler's Museum **89**

66. Soak In a Historical Sleep at the Centennial Inn Bed & Breakfast **90**

67. Appreciate the Talent of a Variety of Artists with Public Art around Holland. **92**

68. Take Time for History (and a Selfie) at the Clock Tower **93**

69. Relive a Historical Shootout at the Warm Friend **94**

70. Muster Up Your Troops at the VanRaalte Farm Civil War Muster. **95**

71. Learn about Life before City Water at the Pump House Museum and Learning Center. **96**

72. Tiptoe through the Tulips at Veldheer Tulip Gardens **98**

• •

73. Say Hello to Dutch St. Nicholas at Magic at the Mill **100**

74. Get inside a Real Working Windmill at Windmill Island Garden . . .**101**

75. Klomp Your Way through Dutch Culture at Nelis'
Dutch Village **102**

76. Enjoy the World's Biggest Tulip Festival at the Annual
Tulip Time Festival **104**

77. Explore Classic and Modern Art at Kruizenga Art Museum **105**

78. Create a Keepsake at Paint a Pot Studio **106**

79. Color Your Way to Fun at Carolyn Stich Studio & Gift Shop **107**

80. Wave Hello to Santa at the Parade of Lights **108**

81. Cruise Past Big Red on the *Holland Princess* **109**

Shopping and Fashion

82. Outfit Your Yard and Home at Seedlings Boutique **112**

83. Reap a Local Harvest at the Holland Farmers Market **113**

84. Get Lost in a Book at Reader's World **114**

85. Treat Yourself to a Nutty Paddle Pop at the Peanut Store **115**

86. Learn to Cook with Flavor at Fustini's Oil & Vinegar **116**

87. Take Home a Piece of Holland's History from the Holland
Bowl Mill **117**

88. Become a Part of the Family at Cento Anni
Custom Woodworking **118**

89. Walk Safely on Snowmelt Sidewalks **119**

90. Support a Local Family Business at Apothecary Gift Shop **120**

91. Purchase a Fair Trade Gift at the Bridge **121**

• •

92. Shrink Your Family Footprint When Shopping at Ecobuns Baby & Co. **122**

93. Knit an Heirloom at Garenhuis Yarn Studio **124**

94. Get All Your Questions Answered at the Holland Area Visitors Bureau **125**

95. Feel Good at Gezellig **126**

96. Step Up Your Fashion Style at Jean Marie's **127**

97. Watch Time Tick By at the Holland Clock Company **128**

98. Benefit Holland and the World by Shopping at B2 Outlet Stores. . .**129**

99. Make a Stop on the Antique Trail at Not So Shabby Marketplace. . .**130**

100. Activate Your Senses at Garsnett Beacon Candle Co. **132**

Suggested Itineraries **135**

Activities by Season **139**

Index **141**

PREFACE

I moved to Holland about 20 years ago and almost instantly fell in love with my new hometown. Holland has an eclectic mix of restaurants and breweries, history galore, and so, so much to keep you entertained. A day, a week, or 20 years in this town and you won't be bored!

After my dear sister-in-law Zona enthusiastically recommended I start a blog, I struggled to find success. I wasn't sure what was next for this middle-aged woman with an almost empty nest, so blogging seemed like a fun new adventure. But it wasn't as easy as I had hoped it would be. I hadn't narrowed in on finding the right audience or finding exactly what I wanted to write about. I had no idea that my very first travel blogger conference would turn into a whole new adventure.

Enter the Midwest Travel Network Conference. I was ready for a fun, new adventure and to meet some experts in the field. Imagine my surprise when I was drawn again and again to the Reedy Press table and asking a million questions of Amanda, who patiently answered them as fast as I threw them out.

Suddenly many thoughts clicked, and all of a sudden, I was reminded of how much I love my very own hometown of Holland, Michigan. The more Amanda and I talked, the more clear it became that I needed to share that love with the world. And thus, *100 Things to Do in Holland, Michigan, Before You Die* was born.

• •

ACKNOWLEDGMENTS

I wish I could write a whole book by itself about all of the people who have helped me in some way while I took on this first book-writing adventure. But my time and space are limited, so here goes.

A big thank-you to the many friends who enthusiastically supported this book. Friends like Dannelle G., who is always, always available to answer questions about the process; Theresa G., who teaches me and inspires me by being exactly who she is; Julie H., who planted the author seed in my brain long ago; Zona, who inspired me to begin a new mid-life adventure; And then there's Heidi from JM, who never failed to dish out a hug and a "how's the booking coming along?" whenever I would see her, which made my day every. Single. Time.

And of course, no acknowledgment would be complete without mentioning every member of my family. My goal is to make my family proud, and I can only hope this little book helps make that happen. Mom and dad, who have always loved me from near and far, my husband Dan, my son Tucker, who happily sent mom off on many adventures and let his friends have a laugh at my pink-haired expense. My four grown kids and their spouses, Lexi and Arthur, Hayden and Whitney, Riley, and Drake, and my two favorite people on the planet, Wayde and Peyton. None of life's adventures would be so sweet without all of you.

• •

Independence Day fireworks
at Kollen Park over Lake Macatawa.

Chips and salsa are the perfect companion to a great Mexican beer or a margarita.

FOOD
AND DRINK

TASTE BLUEBERRY-FLAVORED EVERYTHING
AT BOWERMAN'S BLUEBERRIES

Bowerman's Blueberries have been a staple of the lakeshore community since William and Winifred Bowerman began their blueberry farm in 1954. Now their son Randy and his wife, Carol, operate it. The farm has over 90 acres of Blue Crop blueberries and is home to an on-site farm store and bakery.

Try picking a fresh berry from the bush to pop right into your mouth or shop at the farm from mid-July through mid-August on the north side of Holland. You can also visit Bowerman's on 8th Street—no picking required!

The 8th Street location occupies the building formerly known as Alpen Rose, which closed in 2020. Holland residents mourned the closing of this favorite, but our souls were soothed when Bowerman's moved in. Now home to a sunny, café-style restaurant, Bowerman's is always packed with people happy to treat themselves to a famous Blueberry Donut.

15793 James St.
2 E 8th St., 616-738-3099
realblueberries.com

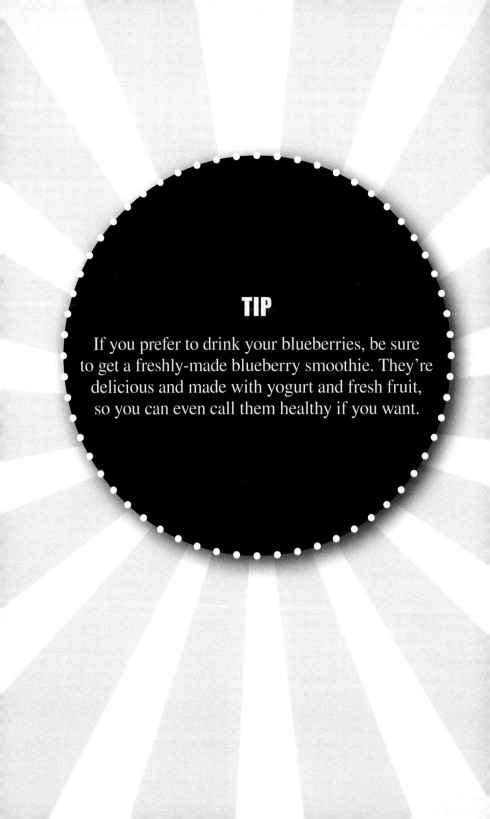

TIP

If you prefer to drink your blueberries, be sure to get a freshly-made blueberry smoothie. They're delicious and made with yogurt and fresh fruit, so you can even call them healthy if you want.

CALL IN YOUR ORDER
AT RUSS' RESTAURANT

When you're craving some good home cooking, head for Russ' Restaurant! Founded by local Dutchman J. Russel Bouws, Russ' has been in business since 1934 and remains in the Bouws family. Eastown Russ' has been located on the unique corner of Chicago Drive and 8th Street since 1946. Over the years, Russ' has expanded to include two additional locations in Holland and nine more throughout Michigan.

In an industry where the median lifespan of a restaurant is 4½ years, Russ' 85+ year run is a bit of a miracle. What's the secret? Everything is cooked from scratch, from the pigs-in-blankets to burger buns and even salad dressings! Even better? Half the booths in the Eastown location are outfitted with old-fashioned corded phones so that you can call your order directly to the kitchen. It is the perfect way to introduce the kids to a working, retro phone!

361 E 8th St., 616-396-2348
210 River Ave., 616-392-6300
1060 S Lincoln Ave., 616-396-4036
russrestaurants.com

TIP

If you're following a sugar-free, gluten-free, or carb-free diet, you'll love the "Cloud Bread" offered at Russ'. Perfect for those who love a good bun but normally can't have it! And don't forget to save room for a sweet treat! Russ' is known locally for their homemade pies and apple dumplings, so go ahead and take a slice or a whole pie home with you!

LEARN
THE SECRETS OF HOLLAND
WITH HOLLAND TASTING TOURS

Prepare yourself for a whirlwind of fun and exciting information on one of our most unique Holland experiences. Your Holland Tasting Tour journey will begin on one end of Holland's downtown and end on the other, and you'll be stuffed full of delicious bites and delightful bits of information in between!

Your tour guide will tell you unique stories of our town's history and architecture while stopping periodically to taste some of our favorite local foods. From made-from-scratch pigs-in-blankets from Russ's to a pizza treat and a Dutch cookie, you won't walk away hungry or bored, although your feet may object if you're not in great shape. You will walk about a mile on your tour, all at a moderate pace over a 3-hour timeframe. But don't worry. You will have plenty of stops to rest and refuel along the way.

616-834-4779
hollandtastingtours.com

TIP

If you aren't ready to walk the mile back to your car at the end of your tour, ask your tour guide when you book where to place a car at the end of your route so you can drive yourself back.

TAKE A BREAK FROM YOUR INNER DUTCH
AT THE CURRAGH IRISH PUB

Take a moment to soak in a little Irish cultural ambience in a town full of Dutch culture and history. Named for the headquarters of Flat Racing in Ireland, The Curragh is a little slice of Ireland right here in Holland and is full of Irish hospitality. In Ireland, the pub is the center of a town's social life, and this little pub in Holland serves this role perfectly.

Come in and enjoy the atmosphere on one of Curragh's regular trivia nights; enjoy a traditional Irish dish like bangers & mash or corned beef & cabbage, paired with a cocktail or an Irish whiskey. You'll find plenty of American options on the menu if you're not into the traditional fare.

If you visit during March, plan to enjoy the annual St. Patrick's Day Parade, which the Curragh participates in every year!

73 E 8th St., 616-393-6340
curraghholland.com

TASTE A TOMMY TURTLE
AT CAPTAIN SUNDAE

If you love ice cream (and who doesn't), you'll love Captain Sundae. Opened in 1980 on the route to the Holland State Park beach, Captain Sundae quickly became a local favorite for high-quality ice cream treats. As the locals embraced the Captain, expansion was inevitable. Twenty-five years after its debut, Captain Sundae opened a second location in the neighboring town of Zeeland in 2005, then the South Holland location in 2006.

Each location is unique and wonderful. Feel like mini golfing? Head for the original north location, where you can putt your way through the Pirate's Landing mini golf course. Are you looking for a great cup of coffee with your ice cream? The South location is just right for you, with your favorite Starbucks drinks on the menu! One thing's for sure: whichever location you favor, you need to try a Tommy Turtle Sundae, unique to the Captain!

365 Douglas Ave., 616-396-5938
247 W 40th St., 616-393-4900
537 W Main Ave., Zeeland, 616-772-1540
captainsundae.net

LISTEN FOR THE WHINNY
AT CRAZY HORSE STEAKHOUSE

In 1997, a legend was born with the opening of Crazy Horse Steakhouse. For over 20 years, this restaurant has valued community. Take a look around the dining room walls, where you will see dollar bills everywhere! The owners periodically collect the money and give it back to those in the community who can use a helping hand.

My favorite part of Crazy Horse (besides the whinny at the door) is the excellent service! Crazy Horse states that hospitality is their passion, which is evident from the moment you enter until the cheerful goodbye as you leave after a great meal! Staff will treat you like an old friend throughout your visit, and that feeling is almost as memorable as their delicious Cowboy Ribeye! But don't worry—if ribeye isn't your thing, you can enjoy a salad, a bowl of their delightful chicken corn chowder, or even a burrito.

2027 N Park Dr., 616-395-8393
crazyhorsesteakhouse.com

TIP
Crazy Horse Steakhouse has given away over a quarter of a million dollars in the 20 years they've been collecting dollar bills from the walls.

INDULGE IN A BACON-FLAVORED DONUT
AT DEBOER BAKKERIJ AND DUTCH BROTHERS RESTAURANT

DeBoer Bakkerij ("bakery" in English) and Dutch Brothers Restaurant is owned by fourth-generation baker Jakob DeBoer and his three sons. Both locations offer bakery items made from family recipes perfected and passed down over generations. One of their crowning achievements is the bacon donut, flavored with maple syrup and topped with a gorgeous slice of bacon! Hungry for a meal inspired by Dutch cuisine? Then head for the north side Three Brothers Restaurant for a bowl of authentic ham and pea soup or some *saucijzenbroodjes* (pigs-in-a-blanket). Want to try it all? Order a sampler plate! With a "Taste of the Old Country," you can sample all the Dutch delights, including a piece of mild gouda cheese.

Don't leave either location without a *krakelingen*! Once you've tasted one of these sweet and crunchy delights, you'll want to stock up! These pretzel-shaped cookies are made from puff pastry and doused in sugar. The sugary glaze dries to a sweet and crispy finish. Yum!

380 W 16th St., 616-396-2253
360 Douglas Ave., 616-396-2253
deboerbakery.com

TIP

DeBoer Bakkerij and Dutch Brothers Restaurant is nicely outfitted with Dutch décor, including a very impressive *bakfiet*, or Dutch box bike.

GET A TASTE
OF THE OLD COUNTRY
AT THE WOODEN SHOE RESTAURANT

The Wooden Shoe Restaurant is perfect for tasting genuine old-school Dutch cooking. It's been open since the early 1990s and housed in the vintage structure that was formerly home to the Wooden Shoe Factory. The current owners have mastered the art of the Dutch breakfast. Begin your meal with a side of *balkenbrij*, a traditional Dutch dish made with hamburger, pork butt roast, and liver, mixed with buckwheat flour, and then flavored with alum and allspice. *Balkenbrij* isn't for everyone, though, and the Wooden Shoe has plenty to choose from if you're not into liver for breakfast. Try a made-from-scratch pig-in-a-blanket, a pork sausage wrapped in savory and flaky bread. And don't leave without a giant cinnamon roll for the whole table to share. These babies are huge and way too much for one person with a normal appetite.

441 US 31, 616-396-4744
woodenshoerestaurant.com

TIP

When you stop in at the Wooden Shoe, you may be in for a wait as this is a popular breakfast and lunch destination in Holland. But don't worry. You can meander through the connected Wooden Shoe Antique Mall and enjoy looking at and even purchasing all sorts of beautiful relics from the past.

CREATE A MASTERPIECE
IN A BOWL AT PEACHWAVE

Peachwave is like an ice cream buffet. Step One: Choose your bowl size (trust me, choose bigger than you think you'll need). Step Two: Pick a flavor from 24 available (made daily). Or pick two. Or three. Heck, go crazy and pick them all! Just remember— you need room for the toppings! Step Three: Toppings. So many toppings (over 70) and such a small bowl. Told ya! Choose from gelato, yogurt, or nondairy soft-serve. If you prefer to drink your creation, have the team whip it up into a float, a smoothie, or a shake. The sky's the limit for options here.

Holland is the world headquarters for this delightful treat as of 2015, when local franchise owner Boyd Feltman bought the trademark and the brand. Peachwave is proud to call beautiful Holland home, and we are proud to call them one of ours.

6 W 8th St., 616-928-0666
peachwaveyogurt.com

TIP
If you like your soft-serve in classic form, you'll have no problem here. All flavors are stocked in two-flavor machines with compatible flavors allowing you to twist to your heart's content. Think strawberry with chocolate or peanut butter with banana.

SAY HELLO TO FRESH FOOD AND FRIENDLY SERVICE
AT WAVERLY STONE GASTROPUB

Waverly Stone perfectly fits the definition of a gastropub in that it serves excellent, high-quality, unique dishes in a pub-like atmosphere. You won't find anything stuffy here, but you will find delicious dishes and drinks!

Like many buildings in downtown Holland, the Waverly Stone Gastropub has a long history, but this one highlights it in its name. Initially built in 1898, the building was faced with Waverly Stone sourced from a local quarry, now retired from that purpose. You'll see this stone on many of the downtown buildings.

But more important than the name or the stone fascia is the meal experience at Waverly Stone. You'll find cuisine fit for the finest appetite and a father-and-son team of chefs passionate about classic, globally inspired food and excellent service. Trust me when I tell you you'll want to come back again and again!

20 W 8th St., 616-392-5888
waverlystonepub.com

CHUG A LOCAL FAVORITE
AT NEW HOLLAND BREWING COMPANY

The New Holland Brewery Company is a local favorite and is becoming a national favorite. New Holland popped onto the scene in 1997 right here in Holland, Michigan, and has been making waves ever since. Over the past 25 years, this local pub has expanded from its original location to include two full-service restaurants, a spirits-tasting room, and two brick-and-mortar stores, all in West Michigan. And you can purchase online, too!

To get a taste of Holland's local beer, which is now sold across the country and worldwide, come down to the 8th Street location. Sip a signature bourbon-barrel-aged Dragon's Milk in a variety of limited edition flavors, or sip one of their signature spirits, including Dragon's Milk Bourbon. Whatever tickles your taste buds, New Holland Brewing Company has something you'll love.

66 E 8th St., 616-355-6422
newhollandbrew.com

TIP

If you'd like a peek at how the brewmasters create your favorite flavor, then call ahead and arrange for a Brewery Tour where you can see the magic behind the process. End your tour with a glass of your favorite brew!

BITE INTO AN MGB BURGER
AT GOOG'S PUB & GRUB

Goog's has been a community favorite since it opened in 2002. My family has spent many evenings with Goog's burgers on our plates. Sadly, after 18 years of serving Holland, Goog's shut down in June of 2020 with plans to open a market store instead. But owner Brad White couldn't disappoint the community entirely, so he added a smaller, scaled-down Goog's to the plans for the new mixed-use building. Eight lucky locals can now live in the apartments in the upper story of the building.

When you dine at Goog's, you may have a short wait for your table. But no worries—now you can shop the market for tomorrow night's dinner while you wait for tonight's table. The connected MGB (meat, grocery, beverage) Market sells many ingredients to make your Goog's burgers at home! One thing's for sure: you will not taste a better burger!

667 Hastings Ave., 616-416-2747
googspub.com

TIP
If you are a fan of green olives, you will love Grammy's Olive Burger. The only thing that makes it better than the special olive sauce is the griddle-fried bun it's served on!

BELLY UP
TO A DELICIOUS BREW
AT THE 205 COFFEE BAR

The 205 is named for its street address on Columbia near downtown Holland and has become a favorite meeting place for Hope students and locals around town. The first thing you'll notice when you approach is the gorgeous mural painted on the slate-gray building. The 205 is unique, but not just because of that artwork.

There's also artwork inside, served as coffee and croissant waffles called "Croiffles." The menu is unique and features favorites such as the Pumpkin soy latte in the fall and a refreshing frozen lemonade with Butterfly Pea Flower Tea in the summer.

Your experience isn't complete at the 205 until you've enjoyed one of the sweet or savory Croiffles, which are served year-round. If you're in the mood for something sweet, I recommend the Homemade Banana Custard, Raspberry, and Cinnamon Roll Croiffle. Looking for savory? Try the Salmon Croiffle for the win!

205 Columbia Ave., 616-610-6861
205coffee.com

TIP

Holland's own Chris Garcia painted the lovely murals on the 205. Mr. Garcia has made his mark all around Holland, so see if you can spot his talent as you wander through the many locations in this book.

PRACTICE YOUR PRONUNCIATION
AT LEMONJELLO'S

Everyday banter about town in Holland is the pronunciation of the name of this delightful coffee shop downtown frequented by Hope college students and businesspeople from the community. Is it Lemon Jell-O's? Or the European pronunciation of *Limonjalos*?

No matter how you pronounce the name, you'll find something you love on the menu. With baked goods (some gluten-free) and a full menu of hot and cold drinks for sipping, including Kombucha, lattes, energy drinks, coffees, and sodas, there is something for everyone at Lemonjello's. My favorite? The "Green Army Guy," with (you guessed it) a tiny green army guy at the bottom of your cup.

My favorite part of Lemonjello's is how they practice sustainability. You won't find any trash cans here because guests are encouraged to leave trash for the employees to sort and recycle. This practice allows them to boast less than one bag of waste disposal daily!

61 E 9th St., 616-928-0699
lemonjellos.com

OTHER UNIQUE COFFEE SHOPS IN HOLLAND

Ferris Coffee
57 E 8th St., 616-777-0990
ferriscoffee.com

Simpatico Coffee Joint
714 Michigan Ave., 616-929-9787
simpaticocoffee.com

Way Cup Café
501 W 17th St., 616-796-0589
4waycup.com

The Good Earth Café
14 E 7th St., 616-396-3061
goodearthcafeofholland.com

Carpe Latte
11260 Chicago Dr., 616-396-6005

Bambu Holland
184 S River Ave., 616-928-0989
drinkbambu.com

Joe2Go LLC
166 E Lakewood Blvd., 616-395-5950
joe2gocoffee.com

KIN Coffee and Craft House
1200 Ottawa Beach Rd., 616-298-8153
kincoffeeandcraft.com

TICKLE YOUR TONGUE
WITH A PREMIUM-CRAFTED SPIRIT
AT COPPERCRAFT DISTILLERY

Coppercraft is an award-winning distillery just a few blocks east of downtown Holland. In 2022, they celebrated their first 10 years in business. As soon as you step inside this warm and inviting space, you'll feel the inspiration behind the concept, which includes a tribute to the hardworking laborers who are the meat and potatoes of Michigan.

Coppercraft Distillery creates award-winning whiskey, gin, vodka, and rum. May I suggest a flight to try before choosing a favorite? The cozy, warm atmosphere welcomes you in and invites you to sit back, relax, and enjoy your cocktail. The friendly and knowledgeable servers are happy to suggest a delightful cocktail and will give you tips to re-create your fave at home. If you don't have a favorite when you arrive, you will when you leave!

184 120th Ave., 616-796-8274
coppercraftdistillery.com

TIP
Coppercraft has proudly partnered with the NFL's Detroit Lions since 2019. Ford Field has six Coppercraft-branded bars in-house, serving both spirits and canned cocktails.

FEED YOUR NEED FOR HASHBROWNS
AT WINDMILL RESTAURANT

The Windmill Restaurant has been serving up a local favorite, the famous Windmill Hashbrown Omelette, since the early 1980s. This diminutive restaurant may be small in size, but it is big in popularity, so you may find yourself getting to know your neighbor while waiting in line for a seat on a mild Saturday morning. But don't worry—your feet will stay dry while you wait, even on the snowiest winter day, thanks to downtown Holland's Snowmelt sidewalks.

The history of the Windmill goes back to the 1940s, when locals dined at the then-named "Hoffman's." The restaurant may have changed hands and names a handful of times over the years, but it has always served up mighty fine breakfast and lunches at all hours! And those dishes all come with delicious home-baked bread and cinnamon rolls!

28 W 8th St., #220, 616-392-2726

STROLL THROUGH WASHINGTON SQUARE
AND DISCOVER THE BISCUIT CAFÉ

Take a little walk off the beaten path through historic Washington Square, and you'll discover several shops tucked into this quaint neighborhood area. But don't leave without stopping for breakfast, brunch, or lunch at the Biscuit Café, where family, food, and great coffee are waiting!

Husband and wife team Rob and Tracy pay special attention to all the items on their globally inspired menu, using fresh, natural ingredients supplied by local farmers whenever available. Their love of food and family come together in their unique menu with classic offerings plus two signature dishes named for their daughters, Lily and Harper Rose. You will love the sunny, open seating in the café and the excellent service.

Finally, savor a locally roasted coffee or espresso, and don't forget to treat yourself to one of the best scones in town before you go. Don't worry if you're too stuffed. Take one (or two) to go!

450 Washington Ave., 616-396-1005
thebiscuitcafe.com

GET YOUR FILL OF FISH
AT BOATWERKS WATERFRONT RESTAURANT

Nestled along the banks of Holland's Lake Macatawa, Boatwerks Restaurant has become a staple restaurant in the community. Because it's open seven days a week, Boatwerks makes the perfect place to enjoy a cocktail and soak up some lakeside summer sun any day. Boaters can cruise by and enjoy the view of the gorgeous patio, rebuilt in 2020, or tie up and enjoy lunch or dinner there.

Boatwerks has been open since 2006 in a building that historically served boat and lake-related businesses. The building has found its true purpose in feeding locals and visitors. Maybe it's the delightful menu of New American fare, which boasts some of the best seafood dishes in town. Perhaps it's the friendly and efficient service. Maybe it's the sun-kissed strangers who arrive by boat and tie up at the nearby dock. Whatever draws you in, you'll be glad you're there.

216 Van Raalte Ave., 616-396-0600
boatwerksrestaurant.com

TIP

Boatwerks has Fish Fry Friday every Friday from February through April. Get all your favorites, including Walleye, onion rings, fries, and cole slaw! Yum!

TASTE THE FINER THINGS IN LIFE
AT BUTCH'S DRY DOCK

Find an evening to set aside your worries and let the troubles of the day and week melt away. Butch's Dry Dock is the perfect place to sit back, relax, soak in the ambience, and let the flavors carry you away. When you make your reservation, ask for a window seat to enjoy the foot traffic hurrying by outside.

Butch's earned the Wine Spectator's Best Award of Excellence (one of only ten in Michigan). With this distinction, they have created a menu that pairs each meal with the perfect drink resulting in a culinary experience you won't forget.

If you would like to narrow in on a favorite wine or learn more about the art of wine tasting, try out a wine-tasting event that will introduce you to many varieties of wine paired with small plates.

44 E 8th St., 616-396-8227
butchs.net

TIP

If you can't get enough wine tasting at Butch's, join him on a Culinary Wine Tour, where you will enjoy exploring the tastes and techniques of your favorite cuisines and wines. Check out butchsculinarywinetours.com for information on upcoming tours.

GET SOME DOWN-HOME
COMFORT PIZZA

For over 70 years, Skiles Tavern has served freshly made, delicious pizzas washed down with some of the best drinks available. Skiles is the perfect place to belly up to the bar for your favorite craft beer or settle into a booth with your favorite dinner companion and a pizza or plate of nachos.

This cute little corner pizzeria opened in 1951 and quickly became a Holland favorite. The restaurant has two sections: a bar and a dining side, although you can get food and drinks on either. Your pizza will arrive at your table cut in squares and served on a piece of cardboard, and you'll get the joy of eating from a paper plate! Parmesan cheese and hot spices adorn the tables in baby food jars with holes punched in the top. The kitschy touches make Skiles a unique and casual place to unwind.

154 E 8th St., 616-396-7836
facebook.com/skilestavern

ENJOY A HISTORIC TASTE OF ITALIANO
AT FRICANO'S TOO

Tucked into a little brick building off the main road in downtown Holland, you'll find a scrumptious little pizza parlor and bar called Fricano's Too. The original Fricano's is in Grand Haven but is so beloved that they have expanded with three more pizzerias. The Holland location opened in 1983 and has developed doting followers over the past 40 years.

Step into Fricano's and notice the red and white checked tablecloths. Pick a seat and order a 12-inch thin-crust pizza, the only thing they serve at Fricano's. You can personalize your pizza with any combination of the five toppings covered in their secret cheese blend and sprinkled with just the right spices. Be sure to pack cash, because Fricano's doesn't take credit cards or checks. They do, however, have an ATM conveniently located in the lobby for those who forget their cash.

174 S River Ave., 616-392-6279
fricanospizza.com

TIP
Ask for your pizza "on cardboard" if you'd like it to be slightly less greasy. The cardboard does a great job of soaking up the extra calories for you!

SIP A CIDER AND TASTE A PIE
AT CRANE'S IN THE CITY

Crane's in the City opened in 2010 and has quickly become a favorite for Holland residents and a destination location for all of West Michigan. The original, family-owned Crane's Pie Pantry is located in Fennville, just 20 minutes South of Holland, and uses fruits grown in their orchards for all of their delicious pies, donuts, and other sweet treats.

This location brings an urban take on Crane's original Pie Pantry. Visitors can enjoy all the small-town goodness of the original location right in downtown Holland. Pick up a whole pie or take a break from your stroll down 8th Street and treat yourself to a freshly made salad, soup, or sandwich, served with your favorite coffee drink or a glass of cider served warm or cold! In the summer, sit on the patio right outside Crane's and enjoy the great outdoor ambience!

11 E 8th St., 616-796-2489
cranesinthecity.com

TIP

In October, travel to the Crane's in nearby Fennville to pick your own fruit and enjoy hayrides and a corn maze or choose the perfect pumpkin for carving.

TASTE AUTHENTIC MEXICAN FLAVOR
AT MARGARITA'S MEXICAN RESTAURANT

The Dutch may have settled Holland, but today's residents are multicultural. And we have plenty of room for all the food! Holland has many Mexican restaurants to enjoy, but the local favorite is Margarita's Mexican Restaurant, located in the South Shore Village.

Don't get confused. Margarita's doesn't serve margaritas! In fact, this family restaurant, named for the restaurant's matriarch, the one and only Margarita Salinas, doesn't even have a liquor license. Margarita and her husband Jose opened the restaurant in 1994 and have been serving excellent Mexican fare from her favorite recipes since then.

Say hello to current owner Alonzo Salinas (and son of Jose and Margarita) when you stop in and know that when the restaurant changed hands, so did the recipes! I recommend the fajitas with a side of rice and maybe a homemade tamale (or two).

495 W 17th St., 616-394-3069
margaritashollandmi.business.site/
?utm_source=gmb&utm_medium=referral

OTHER GREAT MEXICAN RESTAURANTS

El Patron Mexican Restaurant
3333 W Shore Dr.
616-796-8336
elpatronholland.com

Taco+ Bar
220 W 8th St.
616-396-5370
taco-bar.net

Poquito
90 W 8th St.
616-298-2881
poquitoholland.com

Taqueria Vallarta
275 E 8th St.
616-848-7778
taqueriavallartaholland.com

Havana Grill
12059 Felch St., #1
616-399-3466
havanagrill616.net

Taqueria Arandas
98 Douglas Ave., #10
616-377-7468
taqueriaarandasmi.com

Taco Fiesta
11972 E Lakewood Blvd.
616-393-0161
facebook.com/tacofiestainc

Baja Grill
777 Washington Ave.
616-546-3600
bajagrillholland.square.site

Supermarket Rosie
106 W 16th St.
616-392-7877

Tacos El Cuñado
442 Bay Park Dr.
616-298-7225
tacoselcunado6.com

Mi Favorita Grocery
408 Columbia Ave.
616-355-1993
mifavoritagrocery.com

Don Miguel
264 N River Ave., #10
616-796-8555
facebook.com/
donmiguelmexicanrestaurant

Tienda Azteca
2027 N Park Dr.
616-355-7804
taqueriaaztecami.com

The Fat Burrito
3015 W Shore Dr.
616-399-9500
thefatburritorestaurant.com

El Huarache
517 Butternut Dr.
616-510-6024
facebook.com/p/el-huarache-100083066025322

The Knickerbocker Theatre
has a fascinating history.

MUSIC
AND ENTERTAINMENT

PACK A PICNIC
AND PRACTICE
YOUR DANCE MOVES
AT KOLLEN PARK'S SUMMER
CONCERT SERIES

If you're looking for free summer fun, take in a concert at Kollen Park, located just west of the downtown area and sandwiched between the west end of 10th Street and Lake Macatawa.

Every Friday night throughout the summer, get your groove on with a free concert by a different local artist each week. The band will set up in the Clamshell from 6:30 to 8:30 p.m. A food truck is on-site from 5:30 to 8:30 p.m. Who doesn't love a great food truck!? Pack a picnic if you prefer, but remember that alcohol is not allowed at Kollen Park.

All concerts are free, and seating on the grassy area in front of the Clamshell is first-come, first-served. Pack your lawn chair or a blanket, and plan to get comfy. You can even bring the family pup with you as long as he is on a leash while in the park.

240 Kollen Park Dr., 616-394-0000
holland.org/summer-concert-series

SOAK UP
THE LOCAL TALENT
AT HOLLAND COMMUNITY THEATRE

The Holland Community Theatre is a well-loved traditional theater in a community that celebrates the arts. This beloved theater company began in 1960 and has been a constant in Holland's theater scene. The company presents three seasons of performances, one each in spring, summer, and fall. They also offer family-friendly productions with a children's show, a holiday show, and a show cast entirely with teens.

Holland Community Theatre borrowed space from our local high school for performances for years. But in 2019, they purchased and remodeled their current location from what was formerly a church building near downtown, turning it into a theater. This charming space is now home, where they provide quality entertainment and a place for thespians of all ages to grow their skills through volunteering both on stage and behind the scenes.

50 W 9th St., 616-396-2021
thehollandcommunitytheatre.org

THRILL YOUR INNER THESPIAN
AT HOPE COLLEGE REPERTORY THEATRE

A visit to Holland in the summer must include a performance at the Hope College Repertory Theatre, or "The Rep."

The Hope Repertory Theatre was established in 1972 and has entertained and enriched the lives of Holland residents and visitors for over 50 years. Talented students from Hope College's theater department stage multiple productions annually from May through August. If you love theater, you'll enjoy any of these terrific performances, all taking place at various locations on the Hope College Campus.

Stop by the ticket office to see what's playing, or even better, check the website and plan ahead. Because the three venues where productions occur are located on the Hope campus, treat yourself to dinner at one of the downtown Holland restaurants and walk to the show afterward. And don't worry about dessert, because food, drinks, and merch are all available at the show!

141 E 12th St., 616-395-7600
hope.edu/offices/hope-summer-repertory-theatre

TIP

Each summer, theater students from Hope College create a performance perfect for the youngest thespians. These child-friendly productions take place theater-in-the-round style which allows the smallest guest to get in on the action!

FEEL THE HISTORY
OF HOLLAND AT PARK THEATER

The Park Theater's roots extend back to 1886. After its humble beginning as a woodworking mill and feed store, the building eventually became a theater in 1920. Originally used to show movies, the Park Theater is now a nonprofit community staple hosting year-round events.

The Park comes alive with a full schedule showcasing tribute bands, comedy troupes, dinner theater, and many other unique offerings. Once inside, you can satisfy your thirst with a beer on tap from local favorite New Holland Brewing Company or sip a cocktail or your favorite glass of wine. Pizza from Petrino's is also available at most events.

On Tuesdays, hop up on stage to share your talent or cheer on those brave enough to take the stage! Express Yourself Tuesdays include spoken word poetry, music, and comedy from local performers. And mark your calendar for karaoke night on the third Friday of the month!

248 S River Ave., 616-294-3678
parktheatreholland.org

TIP
In 2019, the south wall of the Park Theater was deemed dangerously unstable. The community rallied around the Park Theater and helped fund the $40,000 repair in order to keep the theater up and running.

INCREASE ARTISTIC AWARENESS
AT KNICKERBOCKER THEATRE

Is there a better reason to love the Knickerbocker Theatre than the sound of its name rolling off the tongue? Maybe not, but there is more to this theater than the name. The Knickerbocker has a fascinating history in Holland. Built in 1911, it was not welcomed by conservative residents, who were convinced that a theater would bring ill repute to their town. This idea was confirmed when a co-owner fell and died while hanging the electric sign. Many took it as a bad omen. The opening was delayed for months.

But time and progress have found the Knickerbocker now thriving. Many years later, it is embraced by the local community and has hosted Ted Talks, presidential visits, magicians, movies, and even a performing elephant! Today you can take in an art film, a concert, or any number of stage performances, all sponsored by Hope College.

86 E 8th St., 616-395-7222
hope.edu/directory/buildings/knickerbocker-theatre

FEEL THE FREEDOM
AT THE INDEPENDENCE DAY
FIREWORKS CELEBRATION

Kollen Park sits at the edge of Lake Macatawa next to Boatwerks Restaurant. On Independence Day, the city of Holland hosts a party in the park, perfect for families of all ages. The park has beautiful green space, a clean and well-maintained playground, and plenty of picnic tables. Claim a table or bring a blanket and stay for the day. Many families and groups enjoy tossing a football or frisbee or relaxing in the summer sun.

Once you settle in, enjoy fishing off the Heinz Waterfront Walkway in Lake Macatawa. Hungry? Food carts are available. Sometimes you'll catch a concert, or students from the local martial arts studio will perform. After relaxing in the park during the day, be ready at dusk for fireworks launched from a barge in the water, paired with patriotic music over the park's speaker system.

240 Kollen Park Dr., 616-394-0000
holland.org/independence-day-fireworks

TIP

Come early in the day and park in the lot next to the park. You won't have to haul your chairs and blankets far to get a prime spot for the show. At the end of the fireworks, return to your car in a jiffy, load up, and head out. Post-fireworks traffic is heavy, but the Holland Police Department does a fantastic job directing traffic and clearing the space quickly.

ATTEND AN EVENT
AT HOLLAND CIVIC CENTER PLACE

The Holland Civic Center Place does it all! From hosting headlining comedy shows, big-name musicians, annual expos and sporting events to making space for the yearly Dutch Dancer practice, the Civic Center is always hopping.

Browse through an artisan gift market with countless booths of handmade goods during the holiday season. Watch the schedule for expos and local festivals, including the annual LAUP Fiesta, and Tulip Time events! A favorite for women in the community, Holland Civic Center Place hosts an annual Girlfriends Weekend early each spring, complete with special classes, food, and drinks!

The Civic Center is home to the Holland Farmers Market twice weekly in the summer and the Kierstmarket during holidays. You can even reserve space to use for your private event. The Civic Center is conveniently located at the west end of 8th Street and was recently updated with a more modern exterior.

150 W 8th St., 616-928-2000
hollandciviccenter.com

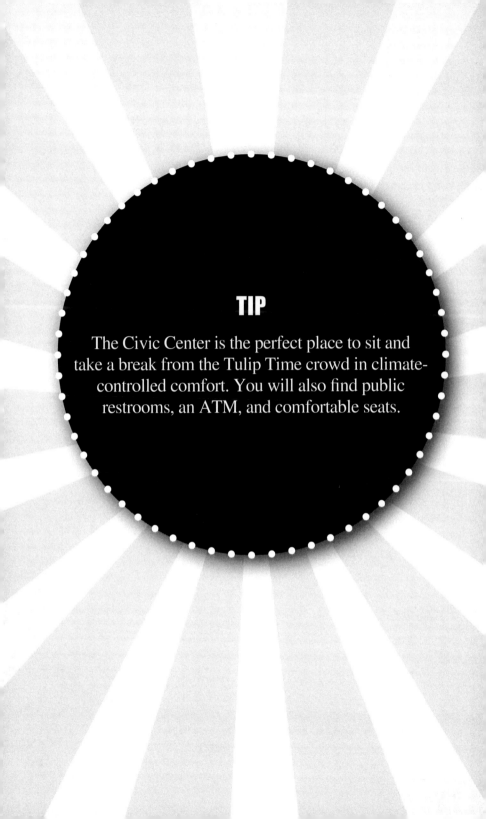

TIP

The Civic Center is the perfect place to sit and take a break from the Tulip Time crowd in climate-controlled comfort. You will also find public restrooms, an ATM, and comfortable seats.

KICK YOUR FEET UP
AT SPERRY'S MOVIEHOUSE

Sperry's Moviehouse, Holland's boutique movie theater, opened downtown in 2019 and boasts luxury recliner seats with built-in heat and massage. Order dinner and have it delivered straight to your seat when you buy your tickets! The menu includes an elevated selection of handhelds, burgers, pizzas, and pasta dishes. Or choose a classic treat of popcorn and candy, all topped off with an all-you-can-drink soda!

If you're bringing a little one to the theater, choose a movie playing in the Playhouse. This family-friendly viewing room is perfect for the latest kids' flic. The side lights remain lit throughout the movie, giving just enough light, so it's safe to move around when the kids get restless. Parents and grandparents love knowing there's a play structure in the theater so kids can safely release some extra energy without missing a minute of the movie.

84 W 8th St., 616-795-0685
sperrysmoviehouse.com

HOLLAND HAS PLENTY OF LOCATIONS TO VIEW A MOVIE. ENJOY ANY OF THESE!

GQT Holland 7
500 S Waverly Rd., 616-392-9547
gqtmovies.com

AMC Holland 8
12270 James St., 616-394-5774
amctheatres.com/movie-theatres/grand-rapids/amc-holland-8

Knickerbocker Theatre
86 E 8th St., #3504, 616-395-7222
hope.edu/directory/buildings/knickerbocker-theatre

PARTY HEARTY
AT THE ANNUAL LAUP FIESTA

The Latin Americans United for Progress (LAUP) has been empowering Latinos to improve West Michigan via education and advocacy and celebrating their unique roles in our community since 1964. The LAUP is open to anyone, welcomes diversity in partnership, and provides many resources, including translation/interpretation services, college advising, and youth programs.

Each year, on one Saturday in July, the LAUP hosts a Fiesta at the Holland Civic Center Place. Over the past few years, attendance has swollen to over 20,000 people, all gathered to celebrate various Latino cultures! This family-friendly event is open to everyone and is the perfect place to celebrate the differences and similarities between cultures, make connections, and enjoy entertainment, authentic food, dancing, music, a carnival, and exhibits highlighting Latino cultures. Be prepared for a great time. Come prepared to learn something new and have a great time!

430 W 17th St., #31, 616-888-7225
laup.org

GET EDUCATED ABOUT AGRICULTURE
AT THE OTTAWA COUNTY FAIR

Every summer, the Ottawa County Fair brings families and the community together to celebrate agriculture and enjoy affordable family fun. Come on out and look at the prize-winning 4H farm animals, enjoy entertainment of all kinds, and even have a beer!

The history of the Ottawa County Fair is just one of its many delights. The fair was born in 1959 when the county took a 50-acre parcel of land that needed attention and used it to host one of the top five fairs in Michigan.

But the Fairgrounds aren't just about the annual fair. Watch the calendar and learn how active these fairgrounds are in our community throughout the year. They participate in Tulip Time events, gather bikers for the annual Blessing of the Bikes, and have recently begun hosting the Holland Celtic Festival and Highland Games.

1286 Ottawa Beach Rd., 616-399-4904
ottawacountyfair.com

TAKE IN
THE LOCAL TALENT
WITH THE SUMMER STREET
PERFORMER SERIES

Walk down 8th Street in downtown Holland on any Thursday in June, July, or August from 6:30 to 8:30 p.m., and you'll get a special treat. Thursdays are the day when the local talent comes out to entertain the town! Bring some loose change and cash to reward your favorites with a tip.

While you meander among the shops on 8th Street, you'll find jugglers, singers, musicians, magicians, and the like, all carefully placed up and down the sidewalks for entertainment. Choose a bench or dine at one of our patio-seating restaurants to enjoy the talent.

Be sure to look for our local favorite, "balloon guy." This young man has been making his way around Holland creating balloon animals for the kids for at least the past 20 years. Holland is known for supporting the arts in the community, and this young man is the perfect example.

Downtown 8th St., 616-394-0000
holland.org/summer-street-performer-series

TIP

Look for local balloon artist Dan Mutschler, who is self-taught and has been making balloons for Holland residents for over 20 years.

STEP INTO THE FUTURE
AT ZERO LATENCY HOLLAND

Holland is the proud home of Michigan's only free-roam virtual reality center. Strap on your gear and join a mission to fight zombies or enter a sci-fi world outside your own.

But what is Zero Latency? Great question! Zero Latency Holland (ZLH) offers a cutting-edge free-roam virtual reality play space for gamers ages 13 and up. And you don't have to be an experienced gamer—some of their regular visitors are middle-aged moms! Once you strap on your headgear, you can wander freely through the 2,000-square-foot arena with up to seven besties and work together to save the world.

Sound fun? Book a time slot on the ZLH website before arriving. Zero Latency's in-house bar and entertainment space make this the perfect place to party! Plan your next birthday or family reunion with them!

2522 Van Ommen Dr., 616-298-8831
zerolatencyholland.com

CELEBRATE A WORLD OF MUSIC
AT THE INTERNATIONAL FESTIVAL OF HOLLAND

Every autumn, Holland allows us to experience cultures from around the world right from our doorstep. You don't need to pack a bag for this international trip. The day begins with a soccer scrimmage at Riverview Field. Then head to Holland's Civic Center to shop, dance, and eat your way through the day.

The kids can celebrate at the children's fiesta, have their festival passports stamped, take part in a Chinese dragon dance, learn African drumming, and create their very own works of art. Adults can sample foods from around the world, including Ethiopia, South America, and Mexico. Bring home a memento of your day with a trinket from your favorite international vendor.

If you'd like to relax and soak in the culture, find a seat near the main stage, where you'll hear the sounds of Native America, Cuba, Africa, and beyond.

150 W 8th St., 616-355-1324
internationalfestivalholland.com

EXPAND YOUR MIND AND YOUR DIGITAL EXPERIENCE
AT HERRICK DISTRICT LIBRARY

Dutch settlers founded the Herrick District Library in 1847. After several moves in its 175-year history, Herrick has called its current location home since 1960 and is an integral part of the Holland community. I have spent more hours than I can count sitting in one of the quiet areas of this library writing the book you have in your hand.

Take an online or in-person class for kids or adults on anything you can imagine: knitting, computers, home improvement, genealogy, basket weaving, or Lego building. Kids will love the turtle tank on the second floor of the main library, where the selection of children's materials and activities is astounding!

Adults will love the vast selection of books, videos, and music available in hardcopy, not to mention the online resources. That's right. You never have to leave your house to check out your favorite book, song, or movie.

300 S River Ave., 616-355-3100
herrickdl.org

LET THE MUSIC TAKE YOU AWAY
AT HOLLAND SYMPHONY ORCHESTRA

Once again, Holland is a small city with extensive offerings, which shows in our very own Holland Symphony Orchestra. Under the leadership of music director Johannes Müller Stosch since 2001, the orchestra attracts visitors from West Michigan and beyond.

The orchestra began in 1989 and has grown to include 100 musicians who perform concerts year-round. In addition, this semi-professional orchestra shows its commitment to enriching our community by sponsoring programs and events for all ages, from preschool to retirement. Opportunities abound for residents of Holland to participate and learn from the HSO, and visitors can enjoy one of the many concerts throughout the year.

The Holland Symphony Orchestra performs its six main performances at the Jack H. Miller Center for Musical Arts, a Hope College concert hall. This 64,000-square-foot building was completed in 2015 and is a work of art deserving of a visit in its own right.

96 W 15th St., #201, 616-796-6780
hollandsymphony.org

The Hope College Flying Dutchman enjoys his march in the Tulip Time parade.

SPORTS
AND RECREATION

PET A PIG OR A PONY
AT FELLINLOVE FARM

You haven't experienced farm life in Holland until you've experienced Fellinlove Farm. This small-scale family farm is open to guests of all ages and all abilities. Come over, enjoy hands-on interactions with the live farm animals, and meet the family!

Owner Cheryl Heidema Kaletka developed Fellinlove Farm to help meet some of the needs of her two adult daughters with special needs. The farm now hosts gatherings, parties, and small groups for education, recreation, and some down-home farm fun with the animals.

Animal residents of Fellinlove Farm include Fell ponies, horses, donkeys, African Zebu cattle, pigs, a hedgehog, a groundhog, dogs, llamas, fish, and more! The farm also hosts an annual prom event for adults from various programs in the West Michigan area that work with those with special needs. Falling in love with Fellinlove Farms doesn't take much!

6364 144th Ave., 616-283-7555
fellinlovefarm.com

SPEND A DAY ON THE LAKE
WITH HOLLAND WATER SPORTS

One of the best ways to spend a summer day in Holland is by the water and on the water. Head over to Holland Water Sports, conveniently located on the way to the State Park and the shore of Lake Macatawa.

If you're looking for a leisurely ride on the water, pack a picnic and rent a pontoon boat that seats 8 to 10 people. If your spirit calls for more adventure, choose a power boat or a jet ski. You can even try out your jet ski on the big lake on a calm day. But there's plenty of space on Lake Macatawa if you prefer calm waters. The staff at Holland Water Sports can advise you on what is safest.

Whichever rental you choose, slather on sunscreen and pack a snack because a day in the sun and water will surely leave you not just wet but also sun-kissed and hungry!

1810 Ottawa Beach Rd., 616-399-6672
hollandwatersports.com

WALK THROUGH A DUNE
AT TUNNEL PARK

Tunnel Park is the perfect place for a family gathering. The park covers 22 acres of land and offers swimming, sunbathing, a large grassy area, and a playground. Climb the dune to get to the sandy beach on the other side, or walk right through it if you please. A unique, short tunnel is carved out through one of Lake Michigan's impressive dunes. The view from the beach side will take your breath away! There's even a small overlook deck at the end of the tunnel for those who don't care to traverse the beach for the sunset.

Tunnel Park offers plenty of parking, a modern restroom facility, a foot-washing station, four sand volleyball courts, a horseshoe pit, and plenty of space to stretch out with a crowd. Reserve a picnic shelter through the Ottawa County Parks Department for a large group gathering.

66 Lakeshore Dr., 616-738-4810
miottawa.org/Parks/tunnel.htm

TIP
When you walk along the beach with water lapping at your toes, look south. On a clear day you'll be able to catch a peek at Holland's Big Red lighthouse in the distance.

GIVE YOUR PEDOMETER A WORKOUT
AT HOLLAND STATE PARK PIER

The best part of walking the Pier at Holland State Park is the view of the channel, the beach, and our famous red lighthouse. The state park has plenty of parking, so you can pull in and stay for a while, soaking up the sun and dipping your toes (or more) into the waters of Lake Michigan.

Take a walk down the pier on the south side of the channel. When you reach the end, look back at the Holland Harbor Lighthouse, known to the locals as "Big Red." Big Red dates back over 150 years to 1870 when federal funds built the first structure at Holland Harbor.

If you're new to the area and recognize Big Red, it may be because she is the inspiration behind Hallmark's 2022 Lighthouse Ornament. You'll want to add this little beauty to your collection.

2215 Ottawa Beach Rd., 800-506-1299
bigredlighthouse.com

SAY GOODNIGHT TO THE SUN
AT HOLLAND STATE PARK BEACH

One of the best things about living near the shore of Lake Michigan is the sunset. I've watched the sunset over the ocean many times, and our Lake Michigan sunsets rival them every time.

Arrive with plenty of time before the sun sets and take a leisurely walk through the soft sand as a romantic date night. Have the kids along? Let them build sandcastles on the beach as the sun dips below the horizon.

Grab a snack or ice cream cone from the on-site Beachplace Café. Or pack a picnic to enjoy the show. Although the Café is closed during winter, the sunset isn't! A winter sunset on a clear night can be just as gorgeous as any summer sunset. Park and watch from the warmth of your car while the sun drops below the horizon, ending another day in West Michigan.

2415 Ottawa Beach Rd., 616-399-9390
hollandbeachplace.com

GET THE BEST VIEW OF LAKE MICHIGAN
ON MT. PISGAH

On your way to Holland State Park, look for the entrance to Mt. Pisgah on your right, marked with a pergola and an informational sign. Park your car about a quarter mile down on the left, just past the ice cream shop.

Get warmed up for the climb as you walk the trail back to the 239 steps that take you to the top! Don't feel rushed. Benches are conveniently placed all along the way up, so sit and take in the view periodically as you make your way. You may receive a cheery hello from a runner zooming past!

Once you reach the top, you will be glad you made the effort! Enjoy 360-degree views of Lake Macatawa, Lake Michigan, and Big Red sitting along the channel. Plan to visit on a full moon night for an incredible sunset over Lake Michigan and a moonrise over Lake Macatawa.

2238 3rd Ave. (approximate)
miottawa.org/parks/beach.htm

STRAP ON
A PAIR OF ICE SKATES
AT GRIFF'S ICEHOUSE WEST

You may think of Holland as a summer beach town, and that's not entirely untrue. But we also have a long list of fun activities to enjoy in the winter. Consider Griff's Icehouse West, where you can learn to skate and play hockey or take a freestyle cruise around one of the two indoor ice skating rinks. Griff's schedule is packed with public skating times, drop-in hockey, and more. They even offer adaptive Learn to Skate classes for those with physical or developmental differences.

But if you're not game for strapping on a pair of skates, come out and watch! Griff's is home to Hope College's hockey team and the West Michigan IceDogs Team, comprised of youth aged 4 to 16.

Griff's is a bit off the beaten path, located on the north side of Holland, but you'll find a visit here is well worth the trip!

4444 Holland Ave., 616-796-6927
griffswest.com

TIP

Griff's West is managed by the owners of the Grand Rapids Griffins, which is an AHL affiliate team of the Detroit Red Wings.

PADDLE YOUR HEART OUT
WITH TULIP CITY PADDLE TOURS

There is no time like now to learn how to enjoy the water from a paddleboard! Beth Felicelli, the owner of Tulip City Paddle Tours, can get you started.

If you're new to the paddling world, sign up for a one-hour beginner class to learn to paddle on Gilligan Lake, a small and quiet lake in Laketown Township. Choose a regularly scheduled class when weather permits, or you can schedule a private lesson. And no worries if you prefer not to stand. Paddleboarding works just fine if you sit or kneel, too!

Once you feel comfortable sitting, kneeling, or standing, attend a Windmill Island Tour to get a unique view of Holland's own DeZwaan windmill from the water! If you're an experienced paddler, you may enjoy an extended tour, which is also available. Keep an eye on the website for an updated summer schedule, or contact Beth to book your tour!

Various Locations in Holland, 616-405-0497
tulipcitypaddletours.com

NURTURE NATURE
AT DEGRAAF NATURE CENTER

The DeGraaf Nature Center is an 18-acre nature preserve that will leave you not wanting to leave! During the school year, DeGraaf works with local school districts to educate children about the history of the area and nature conservation. But you don't need to be an elementary school student to enjoy what DeGraaf has to offer.

Walk one of the numerous nature trails to find upland and lowland forests, a Michigan meadow, and even a pond! The trails are perfect for snowshoeing in the winter, with snowshoes available for rent during business hours.

Not all education is outside, either. The on-site Helen O Brower Visitors Center has a few live residents that love visitors, too. Say hello to amphibians, reptiles, and even owls. You can also get an up-close look at regional taxidermy exhibits. Bring a cup of coffee and enjoy watching the birds at the feeders.

600 Graafschap Rd., 616-355-1057
outdoordiscovery.org/degraaf

DISCOVER THE OUTDOORS
AT THE OUTDOOR DISCOVERY CENTER

From the walking trails to the Cultural History Center and everything in between, the Outdoor Discovery Center (ODC) offers plenty to do for visitors of all ages. The ODC actively promotes activities that motivate adults and children to be active and outdoors.

Even an indoor girl like me can't resist the charms of the Outdoor Discovery Center, so don't worry if you're not a natural outdoor enthusiast. Enjoy Women in Nature programs, catch-and-release fishing, or time at the Nature Play Park or on the beautiful Art Trail. There truly is something for everyone.

My favorite is the Birds of Prey exhibit, home to 12 species of permanently injured or disabled native Michigan birds. They serve an essential purpose in educating visitors and members of the Holland Community and West Michigan. See the resident birds of prey any time you walk the trails open from sunrise to sunset.

4214 56th St., 616-393-9453
outdoordiscovery.org

LISTEN FOR THE PEW PEW OF LASER FIRE
AT THE LOST CITY

Before you can enjoy the fun of the laser tag game that lies deep within the recesses of this 25-year-old business in Holland, you'll need to enter through the unique bricked archway.

You may underestimate the fun you can have in a laser tag video arcade, but let this grandma assure you that there is fun to be had, no matter your age. Once inside, strap on your laser gear and go to battle.

If laser tag isn't your scene, no worries; test your skills on the indoor mini golf course or slip a coin in the slot and play some old-fashioned video games. And when you wear yourself out, sit back, relax, and enjoy a piping hot pizza and a soda.

The Lost City is great for hosting a birthday party, entertaining the grandkids, or having a fun date night!

12330 James St., 616-396-6746
the-lostcity.com

EMBRACE YOUR INNER CHILD
AT BAM! ENTERTAINMENT CENTER

The sound of pins scattering under the force of a bowling ball slamming into them isn't the only thing to capture your attention when you enter BAM! family entertainment center. Your senses will reel with the sound of digital video gaming, the sight of adventurous rope climbers, and the smells of pizza and other bowling alley treats.

Your entertainment possibilities are endless at BAM!. Sign up for a bowling league or reserve an open lane. Celebrate a child's birthday party at the Bitty BAM! lanes, or book the Private VIP suite for an adult-sized party!

But your time at BAM! isn't limited to bowling. Shoot down your enemy in a game of laser tag, test your escape room skills, traverse the high wire course, perfect your axe-throwing skills, rack 'em up for a game of billiards, or relax and sip your favorite drink in the full bar and restaurant.

478 E 16th St., 616-392-7086
gobamgo.com

CHEER ON THE HOME TEAM
WITH A HOPE COLLEGE ATHLETICS EVENT

Holland is the proud home of Hope College, and on any given day you will likely see hordes of Hope students wandering around town. But did you know that Hope College Athletics is a Michigan Intercollegiate Athletic Association member? Or that they belong to the NCAA Division III? How about the 22 varsity sports teams on campus? That's right! And all of these sporting events are open to the public.

Enjoy a winter basketball or volleyball game in the DeVos Fieldhouse or take in a football game at the Ray and Sue Smith Stadium. If you love a great tennis match, join in the fun, cheering on the home team at the DeWitt Tennis Center. All the Hope College Athletics facilities are on Fairbanks Avenue, east of downtown. There's no shortage of opportunities to enjoy your favorite team sport when you're in Holland!

222 Fairbanks Ave., 616-395-7070
athletics.hope.edu

TIP

The Hope College Soccer Stadium is located on the property where Holland's founding father, Albertus C. Van Raalte, lived. At the entrance of the stadium, look for the light-colored brick in one of the red brick pillars, which is a brick from Reverend Van Raalte's original home.

CATCH TONIGHT'S DINNER
WITH A SPORT FISHING CHARTER

Lake Michigan is suitable for a lot more than just sunbathing. Sometimes the best way to kill time is to reel in fish. Don't have a boat? Don't have fishing gear? Don't know how? Don't worry! Check Eldean Shipyard and the Yacht Basin Marina for plenty of fishing charter options.

With an experienced Captain in charge, you can enjoy the sunshine and water, throw back your favorite beverage, and wait for the fish to bite. Be ready to reel him in when you hear the zip of the line! Pack a camera because you'll want to capture it all!

Lake Michigan is chock-full of lake and steelhead trout and salmon, all waiting to come home with you. The charter service will handle all the details, but when you make your reservation, be sure to ask pertinent questions about weather cancellations and what to bring.

Eldean's Shipyard Marina
2223 S Shore Dr., 616-335-5843
eldean.com

Yacht Basin Marina
1866 Ottawa Beach Rd., 616-786-2205
yachtbasinmarina.com

OTHER SPORT FISHING CHARTERS IN HOLLAND

Bachelor One
419-512-5996
bacheloronefishing.com

Beau H2O Excursions
616-901-4764
beauh2oexcursions.com

CoHooker Charter
616-322-2644
chartermichigan.com

Deep V Sportfishing Charters
616-836-9306
deepvsportfishing.com

JJ Sportfishing Charters
616-240-0132
jjsportfishingcharters.com

**Powderhorn
Sportfishing Charters**
616-836-4316
powderhorncharters.com

J.D. Charters
616-550-6248

N' Pursuit Charters LLC
616-889-5706
npursuitcharters.com

**Reel Talk
Sportfishing Charters**
616-215-0865
reeltalksportfishing.com

SuFISHient Charters
616-886-9143
sufishientcharters.com

Unsalted Outfitters
616-836-8063
unsaltedoutfitters.com

**Bending Limits
Sportfishing Charters**
989-464-6546
bendinglimits.com

Black Pearl Sportfishing
517-449-5543
hollandsportfishing.com

HAVE A HANDS-ON SAILING EXPERIENCE
WITH DEEP LAKE VENTURES
SAILBOAT CHARTERS

Care to feel the wind in your hair and the sun on your face, and to smell the fresh air on the water? Charter a sailing experience on Lake Michigan with Deeplake Ventures. Your charter sails out of Eldean's Shipyard Marina or the Yacht Basin Marina and is a beautiful way to get the feel of soaring across the water without the work!

A sailing charter is a great way to celebrate a birthday, anniversary, or special occasion. But why do you need a special occasion to get out on the water? A summer day is a perfect day for a sail! Your chartered sail is customizable and can include a sunset or a leisurely cruise along Lake Macatawa to view the beautiful lakeside homes. Got a need for speed? Captain Jeremy can make that happen with a full-sail-powered journey across the water!

2223 S Shore Dr., 616-403-5491
deeplakeventures.com

OTHER SAILBOAT CHARTERS IN HOLLAND

Nancy Anne Sailing
Yacht Basin Marina
1866 Ottawa Beach Rd., 616-403-3896
nancyannesailingcharters.com

Sailing Mac Charters
Yacht Basin Marina
1866 Ottawa Beach Rd., 616-283-9333

MAKE A SPLASH
AT THE HOLLAND AQUATIC CENTER

The smell of chlorine-filled air tells you water fun is ahead when you enter the Holland Aquatic Center (HAC). HAC has a family-friendly open-swim area, a water obstacle course, swim lessons for all ages, a gym, a rental space for gatherings, and a heated therapy pool. They even host our local high school's swimming events.

If you live in Holland, you'll enjoy a reduced rate to enter the Aquatic Center, but nonresidents are always welcome! Lifeguards are on staff at the Aquatic Center, and generously sized locker rooms are available with plenty of lockers for dry clothes.

In 2022, the Aquatic Center finished a renovation project that began in 2019. The Aquatic Center has so many amenities that the only thing you'll have to worry about when you visit is dragging yourself and your kiddos out at the end when you're done!

550 Maple Ave., 616-393-7595
hollandaquatic.org

FALL ASLEEP TO THE SOUND OF CRASHING WAVES
IN AN UNSALTED VACATIONS RENTAL

An extended stay on the water is a great way to experience Holland. Move in for a season and get a feel for lake life. Unsalted Vacations is Holland's premiere vacation property management company and has thought of all the details. They will walk you through all of the steps of your stay.

Whether you're here for a visit or live locally, a stay on the shore of our unsalted and shark-free Lake Michigan offers an unparalleled beach vacation. Choose a property where you can hear the waves and watch the sun slip into the water on the horizon.

Spend your days in the sun and the water and your evenings around the campfire. You'll get the best sleep ever after a day in the fresh air and sunshine. And when you enjoy an extended stay here at the Lakeshore, you can relax and know it will happen again tomorrow!

332 E Lakewood Blvd., 833-734-0090
unsaltedvacations.com

SHOOSH THROUGH BLANKETS OF SNOW
AT PIGEON CREEK PARK

Fluffy white piles of snow are a tiny bit of what makes winter in West Michigan inviting. Your winter experience in Holland isn't complete until you've rented a pair of skis or snowshoes and explored the trails.

If you don't own cross-country skis, head for Pigeon Creek Park on the north side of Holland, where you can rent them from the Lodge at a reasonable price. Then glide your way around the 10 miles of cross-country skiing trails on the 282 acres of scenic park. Pigeon Creek is family friendly and perfect for skiers of all skill levels. Stop at the information station at the trailhead near the parking lot to choose a trail that suits your skill level.

If gliding through lake-effect snow isn't your cup of tea, or you have the littles along, check out the one-mile snowshoe trail and sledding hill.

12524 Stanton St., West Olive, 616-738-9531
miottawa.org/parks/pigeoncreek.htm

Holland is home to several parks and trails with access for cross-country skiers. Within these parks, you will find over 1,800 acres meant for hiking, biking, snowshoeing, and sledding!

Riley Trails Park
16300 Riley St., 616-738-4810
miottawa.org/parks/riley.htm

VanRaalte Farm Park
1076 E 16th St., 616-355-1057
holland.org/explore-van-raalte-farm-park

Fillmore Discovery Park
5733 142nd Ave., 616-393-9453

Outdoor Discovery Center
4214 56th St., 616-393-9453
outdoordiscovery.org

Huyser Farm Park
Corner of 142nd Ave. and 64th St.

VanBuren Park Dune Trails
16780 VanBuren St., West Olive, 616-738-4810

Saugatuck Dunes State Park
6575 138th Ave., Saugatuck, 269-637-2788

UPDATE YOUR EQUIPMENT HERE:

Uncle Jibs Ski & Kayak Shop
650 Riley St., Ste. F, 616-416-3010
unclejibs.com

RENT AN E-BIKE
AT VELO CITY CYCLES

Holland has over 150 miles of bike trails with views of the beach, the dunes, and the woods. Some routes have bridges, and a few even have spots to stop and fish. Renting an electric bike (e-bike) is the perfect way to explore!

Stop in at Velo City near downtown Holland, rent an e-bike, and let the fun begin! Be prepared to fall in love if this is your first e-bike ride! Riding an e-bike is a creative way to exercise and get out in nature without worrying about those giant hills or running out of steam before heading home.

At Velo City, you can rent for a couple of hours or days. And once you've fallen in love with your e-bike experience, you'll know where to go when you want to add one to your collection!

326 S River Ave., 616-355-2000
velo-citycycles.com

ADDITIONAL OPTIONS FOR BIKE RENTAL

Radventures
321 Douglas Ave., #60, 616-212-3036
radventures49424.com

Cross Country Cycle
345 Douglas Ave., 616-396-7491
crosscountrycycle.com

West Michigan Bike and Fitness
380 Chicago Dr., 616-393-0046
westmichiganbike.com

**Beachside Bike Rental
(in Oak Grove Campground)**
2011 Ottawa Beach Rd., 616-399-9230
oakgroveresort.com

LOWER
YOUR BLOOD PRESSURE
AT WINDOW ON THE WATERFRONT

Did you know that being around water is a natural mood booster? Many scientific studies have shown that just spending time near a body of water is calming, can lower your heart rate and blood pressure, and help you feel more relaxed.

What could be better than gazing at the water? How about walking near it and enjoying the gorgeous view? At Window on the Waterfront, you can do both. Come in late spring and you'll see thousands of tulips in bloom. The view of the DeZwaan windmill is stunning any time of the year.

The entrance to Window on the Waterfront is located on 6th Street in the downtown area. Parking is free, and the views are spectacular on the walking path that follows the waterfront. Make time while you're here to check out the overlook, where you can enjoy watching the local wildlife.

85 E 6th St., 616-394-0000
holland.org/outdoor-recreation/parks/window-waterfront

TIP

At the time of this writing, the City of Holland is developing plans to add a Community Ice Skating park at Window on the Waterfront. Keep your eyes open for construction on this new amenity.

OGLE THE OUTDOORS
ON HOLLAND'S NATURE TRAILS

Holland has abundant natural beauty with over 1,800 acres of hiking and biking trails that wind through the woods, beside the water, and over the sand. These trails are just one of the many incredible ways to get outside, clear your head, get your heart pumping, and enjoy nature. Young nature lovers, couples, solo travelers, parents, and grandparents will all find the perfect route to discover the great outdoors along one of West Michigan's premier lakeshore towns.

Stop downtown at the Holland Visitor Center for a printed map showing the area's many trails, or log on to the State website to choose a route and plan your adventure. Holland's trails can take you down a manicured path, up a sandy dune to climb, or along a paved bike path to explore new places and scenery! You never know what might be waiting around the next corner.

michigan.gov/visittrails

Watch a demonstration of how wooden shoes are made at Veldheer Farms Tulip Gardens.

CULTURE
AND HISTORY

SLEEP ABOVE THE ACTION ON 8TH STREET
AT TEERMAN LOFTS

If you need a place to stay when you visit Holland, consider renting a historic Teerman Loft on 8th Street. The Lofts, named for one of the oldest business families in Holland, remain after Teerman's Department Store closed in 2021 after eight decades of business in Holland. The Teerman name lives on with the lofts above what is now partially occupied by Dutch Village Downtown.

The six luxury suites, named for the five Great Lakes and our local Lake Macatawa, are situated on the second and third floors of the building and are fully furnished with all the amenities you could desire. Each loft features windows across the front to let in daylight and give a view of what's going on below on Holland's bustling 8th Street. These lofts are perfect for either a short or extended stay, whether you're vacationing or visiting for business.

20 E 8th St., 855-833-7626
teermanlofts.com

SURROUND YOURSELF WITH ARTISTRY
AT THE HOLLAND AREA ARTS COUNCIL

There is something naturally compelling about the Holland Area Arts Council gallery. The first thing you'll notice when you visit is the feeling that things are happening here!

And indeed, they are. All the time! This organization supports the arts in all forms. On any given visit, you may find the sound of music, the sight of dancers at work, or the beautiful mess of a visual arts creation under construction.

Staff and volunteers welcome kids and families, experienced or not, to come on in and explore their inner artists. Take a class and try sculpting, learn how to make watercolors pop, or express yourself while learning how to work with mixed media.

The gallery is open daily (except for Sunday) for walk-in visitors, so stop in to see the current exhibition. And don't be surprised if you feel drawn to come back again and again.

150 E 8th St., 616-396-3278
hollandarts.org

FIND YOUR INNER ARTIST
BY PAINTING AND HIDING ROCKS

Keep an eye peeled when you're in Holland, and you might be lucky enough to find a tiny snippet of local art hidden where you least expect it. Holland's locals love to paint small rocks and hide them around town in hopes of bringing a smile to a stranger.

If you're lucky enough to find a rock, be sure and head to the "Holland Rocks Michigan" Facebook page to post a photo. Then re-hide it for someone else to find. We love it when our rocks end up somewhere else in the country or the world, so if you're visiting, go ahead and take that rock with you to re-hide elsewhere.

You can get creative and create some of your own painted rocks. Acrylic paint and any rock will do. Then label your rock with "Holland Rocks Michigan" Facebook group so you can track where your rock travels!

Everywhere in Holland
facebook.com/hollandrocksmichigan

TIP
This very author is the person behind the rocks. My then-10-year-old son and I created the Facebook group in 2017 and painted and hid the first pile of rocks around Holland.

FOLLOW
THE YELLOW BRICK ROAD
TO THE HOLLAND OZ EXHIBIT

Everyone loves *The Wonderful Wizard of Oz*! And everyone loves Holland, so this is a perfect match. The Wizard's creator, L. Frank Baum spent many summers vacationing right here in Holland at Macatawa Park, so it is only fitting to pay tribute to his outstanding contribution to American literature with this exhibit.

The Wizard of Oz Sculpture Exhibit consists of two parts: the bronze statues of your favorite characters from the story frolicking along the north side of the Herrick District Library and the living mosaic book standing in all of its fanciful glory. Each summer, the 10' × 12' book moves out of the city greenhouse and comes alive in Centennial Park, just across from the library. Made of thousands of live plants with a winding path leading right to it, this open book begs to be viewed and photographed. The best part? It's free!

Living Mosaic Book
Centennial Park
250 Central Ave.

Bronze Statues
Herrick District Library
300 S River Ave.

holland.org/oz-sculpture-garden

TAKE A WALK
DOWN MEMORY LANE
AT THE HOLLAND MUSEUM

Look for the light gray building with statuesque pillars just across from Centennial Park. That gorgeous building just around the block from 8th Street is the Holland Museum. Our museum has much to offer, but my favorite part is that it tells the story of Holland's past, complete with relics and stories of the original settlers.

Look for the Holland Medal of Honor interactive display. Holland is home to four award recipients and is one of only two cities in the country to hold this distinction. When you've finished exploring all of the exhibits inside the museum, take a walk around Holland with a virtual walking tour. Learn about Holland's architecture and the Holland fire that happened on the same day as the Great Chicago Fire. You can even tour Pilgrim Home Cemetery, where many of our founding fathers and prominent community members rest.

31 W 10th St., 616-796-3329
hollandmuseum.org

STAND IN THE SHOES OF HOLLAND'S EARLY RESIDENTS
AT THE CAPPON HOUSE & SETTLER'S MUSEUM

Tucked into a quiet neighborhood not far from Holland's downtown are two small homes that pack a powerful punch. The Cappon house was built in 1874 for Holland's first Mayor, Isaac Cappon, and demonstrates what life might have looked like for a family of affluence in the early years of Holland's establishment.

Also steeped in Holland's history is the Settler's House, which sits adjacent to the Cappon House. Multiple working-class families called the Settler's House home in its active years. Although Holland residents built both homes in the same era, the stories behind them represent two very different lifestyles.

The Holland Museum has taken great care to maintain the original integrity of these two homes, and a tour through them will leave you with a better understanding of what it may have felt like to live in Holland during those early years.

228 W 9th St., 616-796-3329
hollandmuseum.org/venue/cappon-house
hollandmuseum.org/venue/settlers-house

SOAK IN A HISTORICAL SLEEP
AT THE CENTENNIAL INN BED & BREAKFAST

A great visit calls for a great place to stay, and with the Centennial Inn Bed & Breakfast, you'll get both, along with a delicious breakfast to start your day right!

Situated on a quiet corner on the campus of Hope College, the historic Centennial Inn was built in 1889 and is within walking distance of the beautiful downtown area. This charming inn, covered in classic red brick and fieldstone, is the perfect place for parents staying in town to visit their college student or a family coming in for Tulip Time.

This charming inn provides a light continental breakfast and has convenient self-check-in. Streaming technology is available in every room, so visitors can log in to their streaming services and feel at home. Private bathrooms for each room and AC and heat will keep you comfortable during your stay.

8 E 12th St., 616-594-0574
centennialinnholland.com

TIP

For an unusual and delicious Tulip Time treat, look for the Fat Ball food cart, usually stationed near Centennial Park. Any local will be able to point you in the right direction. A Fat Ball is a big ball of fried dough stuffed with cream or fruit filling. In Dutch, they are called *oliebollen, vet ballen, smoutebollen,* or *oliekoecken.* Yum!

APPRECIATE THE TALENT OF A VARIETY OF ARTISTS
WITH PUBLIC ART AROUND HOLLAND

Holland isn't all about shopping, tulips, and Dutch culture. We are also about celebrating artistry, education, and community.

Visit Holland.org, download an Art & Architecture Guide, and tour the town looking for 20 unique works of art showcased in the guide, although these are just a sampling of what Holland offers. Look for sculptures created of scrap metal by Stuart Padnos, of steel by local artist Dennis Foley, or of limestone by Jason Quigno, along with several bronze pieces by various artists.

Beyond the printed list, look for several murals painted by local artist Chris Garcia and watch for Benjamin Franklin in bronze. Play a chess game on a life-sized wooden chess set, make a wish in the living coral rock fountain in Centennial Park, and honor the women of World War II in Back Home Brigade, a mural by Jessica Miller.

Various locations, 616-394-0000
holland.org/public-art-around-holland

TAKE TIME FOR HISTORY (AND A SELFIE)
AT THE CLOCK TOWER

In the late 1800s, the newly built Clock Tower building housed the City State Bank. Today the building holds a retail store on the street level and offices on the upper levels. One thing that has remained constant is the large clock face that sits high above street level.

Today we check cell phones for the precise time. Historically, the clock tower served a similar purpose and set a universal time, so men of Holland wouldn't be late for work. A young entrepreneur named John Raven proposed adding the clock to the bank building for this purpose and promised it wouldn't cost the bank a nickel. Local factories and businesses got on board with the plan and funded the tower.

By the mid-1980s, the tower needed some TLC. Holland residents Ed and Elsa Prince purchased the building, leading to its detailed restoration.

190 S River Ave.

RELIVE
A HISTORICAL SHOOTOUT
AT THE WARM FRIEND

Put your fingers in the holes on the exterior wall of the Warm Friend in downtown Holland to get the feel of some real-life history.

The result of a 1932 bank robbery at the First State Bank across the street, these bullet holes give the already historical building extra gravitas. The Warm Friend, now home to seniors, was initially constructed by the Holland Furnace Company in 1925. It carried the slogan "Holland furnaces make warm friends," and served as a hotel and tavern through 1981, when it was re-purposed as a senior living facility.

The bank robbery and resulting bullet holes on the west side of the building are just a tiny part of the unique history of Holland's downtown area. During spring 2022, a worker mistakenly patched some holes during routine maintenance until a passing citizen stopped the work. Three holes remain visible.

5 E 8th St.
resthaven.org/the-warm-friend

MUSTER UP YOUR TROOPS
AT THE VANRAALTE FARM CIVIL WAR MUSTER

Each September, Holland's historic VanRaalte Farm Park transforms into Union and Confederate territories to revisit life during the Civil War. This exciting weekend is an experience like no other here in Holland. So, muster (gather) up your family and step back in time.

On muster weekend, look for hordes of men and women dressed in period clothing and spread out over the 11 acres of the original VanRaalte farmland. On Saturday, you can meander through the encampments where civilians mingle and cook over open fires. Meet Abraham Lincoln, Generals Robert E. Lee and Stonewall Jackson, and other Union and Confederate soldiers. Say hello to Harriet Tubman, watch military drills, and even enjoy a drink at the authentic Civil War–era saloon.

On Sunday, take in a period church service and prepare for the big battle in the afternoon. Bring a camera and plan on having a great time!

1076 E 16th St., 616-399-9390
vanraaltefarmcivilwarmuster.com

LEARN ABOUT LIFE BEFORE CITY WATER
AT THE PUMP HOUSE MUSEUM AND LEARNING CENTER

You can't miss the Historic Ottawa Beach Pump House Museum and Learning Center as you make your way out to Holland State Park. This unassuming brick building is small but packed with great information about the history of the Ottawa Beach area, including an exhibit about our famous Big Red lighthouse.

The Pump House was initially constructed in 1901 as an electric power plant to provide electricity for the Ottawa Beach Hotel. When the hotel burned in 1923, the building became a water-pumping facility for the cottages in the Ottawa Beach area. In the late 1980s, public utilities took over providing water to the locals, and the little pump house was no longer needed.

Skip ahead to the 2010s, and after years of disuse and disrepair, the Historic Ottawa Beach Society, in collaboration with Ottawa County, restored and turned the building into the museum we enjoy today.

2282 Ottawa Beach Rd., 616-607-6854
historicottawabeachsociety.org/pumphouse-museum

TIP

The Museum is open on weekends only from 11 a.m. to 3 p.m. in June and from 11 a.m. to 3 p.m. daily from July 1 through Labor Day. Admission is always free at the Pump House Museum, but donations are welcome.

TIPTOE THROUGH THE TULIPS
AT VELDHEER TULIP GARDENS

In 1950, Vern Veldheer began a tulip farm on the north side of Holland with 100 red tulips and 300 white tulips. Over 70 years later, Veldheer Tulip Gardens is the home of over five million tulips planted in sections and rows for visitors to tiptoe through every spring. The best time to see the tulips is with a visit at the end of April through mid-May. You can even order some bulbs to be mailed to your home in time to plant them in the fall.

Although Veldheer is busiest in the spring, it's open all year. See the only Delft factory in the US that makes Delft pottery from the first mold to the end product, painted with beautiful blue and white images and glazed to perfection. While you're here, see how authentic wooden shoes are made with amazing vintage machines over 100 years old.

12755 Quincy St., 616-399-1900
veldheer.com

TIP

Don't leave Veldheer without wandering over to the buffalo field to look at the 19 American Buffalo that call the farm home. You can even take grass-fed, hormone- and antiobiotic-free bison meat home with you for your next home-cooked meal!

SAY HELLO
TO DUTCH ST. NICHOLAS
AT MAGIC AT THE MILL

The magic is at the Mill for the first three weekends of December. The DeZwaan Windmill, that is. Mark your calendar and head for Windmill Island to see the magic of a Dutch-themed Christmas under lights.

Magic at the Mill boasts thousands of LED tulips set in rows around the main feature, DeZwaan herself! Not to be outdone by the tulips, she is also outlined in beautiful lights. Everything comes together with a synchronized musical light show featuring beautiful holiday music.

Look for Instagrammable moments in front of the windmill and the many shops on-site. Be sure to ride the carousel and watch for a few special treats you'll only see during the holiday season! And don't leave before you say hello to Sinterklaas, who comes each evening to visit and spread Christmas Cheer!

1 Lincoln Ave., 616-355-1030
holland.org/magic-mill

TIP

Buy your tickets as soon as they go on sale in the fall. For the health and safety of everyone, the number of tickets available is limited to ensure an enjoyable experience for everyone!

GET INSIDE A REAL WORKING WINDMILL
AT WINDMILL ISLAND GARDEN

A visit to Holland isn't complete without a tour of our historic windmill. DeZwaan was brought here from the Netherlands in 1964 and was the last windmill exported from the Netherlands. DeZwaan is 250 years old and continues to grind locally grown grain into high-quality flour. You can even stop by the gift shop and grab a bag of flour to take home.

DeZwaan reaches 125 feet from the ground to the top of the blades and lies among 36 acres of beautiful gardens. But DeZwaan is even more unique as home to the only female master miller in the world. Ms. Alisa Crawford is a member of the Professional and Traditional Grain Miller's Guild, which consists of 45 members, 44 of whom are men.

1 Lincoln Ave., 616-355-1030
cityofholland.com/471/windmill-island-gardens

KLOMP YOUR WAY THROUGH DUTCH CULTURE
AT NELIS' DUTCH VILLAGE

In 2022, the Nelis family celebrated 100 years of running this family business in Holland! And that's quite an accomplishment. You can't come to Holland without knowing that Dutch Village is the place to visit in the spring and summer.

During your visit, learn to Dutch dance, ride a Dutch swing chair ride, listen to an authentic Amsterdam street organ, pet various farm animals, and even enjoy some Dutch cuisine. In recent years, the Nelis family has added to the fun with a pirate water balloon battle, a PlasmaCar track for the youngest visitors, and Harry's Windmill ride, a 1940 vintage Ferris wheel restored and fully functional!

Don't leave Dutch Village without Dutch cheese, a stroopwafel, or a wooden tulip. And if you're looking for photos to remind you of your day, you will find plenty around the park. Be sure and look for the Giant Stork. It's a classic!

12350 James St., 616-396-1475
dutchvillage.com

TIP

If you don't have a whole day but really want to take home a few goodies from your visit to Holland, stop in at Dutch Village Downtown on 8th Street, where you will find a whole selection of goodies that represent Holland, Michigan, without the entrance fee to Dutch Village.

ENJOY THE WORLD'S BIGGEST TULIP FESTIVAL
AT THE ANNUAL TULIP TIME FESTIVAL

Each year during the first full week of May you can don your wooden shoes and klomp down to downtown Holland to tiptoe through over 12 miles of tulips of every size, shape, and color. This world-famous tulip festival brings over half a million visitors to Holland annually.

During Tulip Time, treat yourself to Dutch foods, customs, and everything Dutch. Holland rolls out the welcome mat for the visitors and greets them with their always-present friendliness. Each year the north parking lot of the Civic Center is overtaken by the traveling carnival. Enjoy Dutch dancing in the streets at scheduled times each day, and take in a world-class show with artists such as Girl Named Tom and Sara Evans.

The town is bustling throughout the week, with activities for all ages, including not one but three parades. See you there!

42 W 8th St., 616-396-4221
tuliptime.com

EXPLORE CLASSIC AND MODERN ART
AT KRUIZENGA ART MUSEUM

The Kruizenga Art Museum is a teaching museum on the campus of Hope College, but their mission goes beyond educating the staff and students of Hope. They also strive to be an educational resource for the entire West Michigan area. The public is welcome, and the museum often hosts group visits with local students.

The museum, which opened in September 2015, houses the permanent collection of art belonging to Hope College. The art inside the building is compelling, and the outside inspires as well. Inspired by an artist's palette, the oval-shaped building sits in the middle of a lovely sculpture garden that continues to develop.

With 15,000 feet of space, the museum is bright and airy and has plenty of room for both temporary exhibitions and permanent displays. Keep an eye on the schedule; you may be lucky enough to attend a lecture, film, concert, or performance.

271 Columbia Ave., 616-395-6400
hope.edu/arts/kam

CREATE A KEEPSAKE
AT PAINT A POT STUDIO

Love to get in touch with your inner artist but don't love the mess? Then Paint a Pot is the place for you! This unique little boutique-style shop is down-home friendly and tidies up after you! It's perfect for a rainy day or a birthday party.

The process is simple. Come in, pick a piece of pottery, choose your colors, and get busy painting. The friendly staff will answer any of your questions and guide you through the process. The selection of pottery changes, but you will always find something unique to paint. From dishes to décor, there's something for everyone!

But beware! You won't be able to take your masterpiece home with you right away. You'll need to return in a week to pick it up after it's fired. The best part is seeing your work come alive in bright, shiny color when you pick it up!

390 E 8th St., 616-355-6442
paintapot.net

COLOR YOUR WAY TO FUN
AT CAROLYN STICH
STUDIO & GIFT SHOP

The first thing you'll notice when you walk into the Carolyn Stich Studio is the abundance of cheer and the bright colors to accompany it. Carolyn is a long-time Holland resident and a two-time "Art in Bloom" poster winner for our annual Tulip Time Festival.

She now shares her talent with the local community in a number of ways, one of which is by offering her artwork in the form of books, puzzles, greeting cards, framed prints, and pillows in her gift shop. But she doesn't stop there.

A true artist at heart, Carolyn shares her talent and her studio with those who would enjoy getting in touch with their inner artist. Visit the shop during business hours to enjoy an open coloring session, or plan a private event to create some great memories along with your very own work of art.

29 W 8th St., #100, 616-298-2687
carolynstich.com

WAVE HELLO TO SANTA
AT THE PARADE OF LIGHTS

Downtown Holland is aglow with Christmas Cheer around the holidays. Is there any better way to begin the holiday season than with a welcome parade for Santa? Join the families who line up along 8th Street to watch 75 floats, antique cars, marching bands, walkers, and local businesses as they begin at the intersection of 8th and Columbia and march west down 8th Street, ending at the Holland Civic Center, where the *Kerstmarkt* (Dutch Christmas Market) sits. But what makes this parade unique? The lights, of course! Because it takes place in the evening, everyone marching is bedecked and bedazzled in cheerful Christmas lights! From Out On The Lakeshore's lighted rainbow trees to the local Low Carb Grill restaurant staff dressed as bacon, butter, romaine, and other carb-friendly foods, you will see something that makes you smile! The Parade of Lights happens on the Tuesday following Thanksgiving.

8th St.
holland.org/parade-lights

CRUISE PAST BIG RED
ON THE *HOLLAND PRINCESS*

Spend any time near Lake Macatawa or Holland State Park and you will surely notice this gorgeous 65-foot Victorian-style paddle-wheel riverboat cruising by. You'll be on the riverboat if you're one of the lucky ones!

All summer long, from May through October, this beauty cruises from its home on the north side of Lake Macatawa out the channel into Lake Michigan and past historical landmarks and stunning lakefront homes.

Catch some sun on a lunch cruise or watch the sun dip below the horizon on a dinner cruise. Gather 30 of your closest friends and charter the *Holland Princess* for your private party! Plan to belt out your favorite tunes together using the boat's onboard karaoke system or watch the Tulip Time fireworks from the deck of the *Holland Princess* each May.

290 Howard Ave. (Dunton Park), 616-393-7799
hollandprincess.com

Visit Carolyn Stich Studio
in downtown Holland.

SHOPPING AND FASHION

OUTFIT YOUR YARD AND HOME
AT SEEDLINGS BOUTIQUE

What's inside Seedlings Boutique is as compelling as what's outside! Seedlings Boutique is just the place to stop if you need to exercise your creativity, outfit yourself with something new, pick up a hostess gift, or update your home décor. You can even get a new hot tub and accent it with just the right vintage accessory.

Mary Jo, the owner of Seedlings, has taken her love for the creative, combined it with her longtime family business in the hot tub market, and turned it into a charming destination store. Seedlings sells hot tubs, handmade jewelry, yard art, clothing, and vintage items. It's an eclectic selection, but it works!

Seedlings Boutique is a distinctive part of Holland's landscape, just beyond 8th Street where the "North Side" begins. You'll know you've found Seedlings when you see the building surrounded by yard art.

128 S River Ave., 616-392-4221
seedlingsboutique.com

REAP A LOCAL HARVEST
AT THE HOLLAND FARMERS MARKET

Get your fresh, locally grown produce at the Holland Farmers Market. It's fun for the entire family, and you'll find fresh produce, plants, and locally made foods. The Farmers Market is at the 8th Street Market Place in front of the Civic Center and is open every Wednesday and Saturday from 8 a.m. to 2 p.m. from spring through October. Enjoy the free weekly Market Chef cooking demonstration every Saturday and free kids' activities every Wednesday. In October, enjoy professional pumpkin carving! Bring cash, but leave your pup at home as no dogs are allowed. Parking is easy and the market is fully accessible.

Before Christmas, the farmers market becomes the *Kerstmarkt* (Dutch for "Christmas Market"). Local artisans and specialty shops offer their wares to shoppers in 18 winterized and holiday-bedazzled booths. In the style of European Christmas markets, the booths can be easily disassembled and stored away for reuse each season.

150 W 8th St., 616-355-1138
hollandfarmersmarket.com

GET LOST IN A BOOK
AT READER'S WORLD

If you don't follow Reader's World on social media, you should. The dedicated employees of this historic downtown shop do a great job of creatively representing all the things we love about them.

Reader's World has been a part of the downtown Holland landscape since 1967, when it was first established on the corner of 8th and River. After over 50 years of keeping Holland in the know, imagining any other shop where I would want to buy my favorite books is impossible. And with a 20 percent discount on all *New York Times* Bestsellers, why would you go anywhere else?

The store is small, but its imprint on our community is huge. With a vast selection of every kind of book, you should always plan to take your time combing the shelves looking for the perfect next read. And if you can't find it, ask! Special orders are always welcome.

194 S River Ave., 616-396-8548
readersworldbookstore.com

TREAT YOURSELF
TO A NUTTY PADDLE POP
AT THE PEANUT STORE

The Holland Peanut Store is famous in Holland, but not just for peanuts. The Peanut Store began selling vegetables in 1902. Over the years, they switched gears to a soda shop and eventually to its current status as one of the best candy stores in Michigan!

A unique treat at the Peanut Store is the original Nutty Paddle Pop, a vanilla ice cream bar double-dipped in milk chocolate and covered in salty chopped peanuts. If you're not into peanuts, you can have yours plain!

While you snack, notice the college flags on the walls. A lone Hope College flag was the first to fly in tribute to the owner's alma mater. When a customer asked where his favorite flag was, the owner smiled and told him if he brought the flag, he would fly it. A tradition was born! All of the flags you see are donated by customers.

46 E 8th St., 616-392-4522
hollandpeanutstore.com

LEARN TO COOK WITH FLAVOR
AT FUSTINI'S OIL & VINEGAR

Are you a cook or a wannabe cook? Then you're going to love Fustini's Oil & Vinegar! Taken from the Italian word fustino, meaning "drums," Fustini's is named for the stainless steel containers lining the shop's interior. Come on in and sample one of the many flavors of extra virgin olive oil (EVOO) and balsamic vinegar.

Once you've picked a favorite, take some home to experiment. Or, if you need a little guidance, sign up for one of their trendy cooking classes, where you'll learn from an experienced local chef from the Holland Community. When your class is complete, celebrate your accomplishment with the fine meal you've just created! A Fustini's cooking class makes a perfect date night or has the power to plump up your regular menu.

When you stop at Fustini's, ask about their frequent buyer program, which works for in-house and online purchases!

24 E 8th St., 616-392-1111
fustinis.com

TAKE HOME A PIECE OF HOLLAND'S HISTORY
FROM THE HOLLAND BOWL MILL

The Holland Bowl Mill's roots date back to 1926, when Chester VanTongeren opened the original Wooden Shoe Factory on 4th Street. After faithfully serving the community as a unique tourist destination, The Wooden Shoe Factory closed in 1999 when tourism had dropped to a new low. CEO Dave Gier, Chester's grandson, continued the legacy by focusing on producing sustainable, high-quality, one-of-a-kind, heirloom wooden bowls now sold worldwide.

Since 2000, the Holland Bowl Mill has created these bowls while rigorously focusing on sustainability. Wood shavings are re-purposed as horse bedding and small scraps as candlesticks, utensils, and decorative trees. The Mill is a zero-waste company, so you can shop here knowing your shopping will preserve the environment, not destroy it.

When you visit, take a free tour of the mill and be sure to ask about the one-of-a-kind lathe used to create all of the bowls at the bowl mill.

120 James St., 616-396-6513
hollandbowlmill.com

BECOME A PART OF THE FAMILY
AT CENTO ANNI CUSTOM WOODWORKING

Cento Anni means 100 years in Italian, which is the foundational idea behind this unique shop. Each intentionally crafted item the Cento Anni team produces is a work of art meant to serve you today and speak for you tomorrow as you hand it down for generations. Whether an item is created from a client's vision or formed from a scrap of wood left over from another project, each piece is unique and tells a story. And part of that story is told through Cento Anni's locally sourced wood and their practice of zero waste.

Work with the team to create your hand-crafted piece of furniture, or pick up a unique memento to help you celebrate the moments of your life. One step into this storefront and workshop, and you'll instantly feel a part of the Cento Anni family.

136 E 6th St., 616-566-1501
centoanni.com

WALK SAFELY
ON SNOWMELT SIDEWALKS

One of Holland's most impressive features is invisible. But on any winter's day when the snow and ice are covering the streets and sidewalks everywhere, look around downtown and you will see clear walking paths up and down 8th Street and several other areas throughout town. Once you notice, you'll always know it's there!

Maintained by Holland's Board of Public Works (BPW), North America's most extensive municipal snowmelt system is in Holland. Water is heated using waste heat from power generation and pumped through plastic tubing under the streets and sidewalks. The power of this technology can melt an inch of snow every hour, meaning no plows or salt on those roads or sidewalks. There is no place better than Holland to catch some great fresh air and walk safely, thanks to the snowmelt system!

Various locations in Holland, 616-394-0000
holland.org/snow-free-holland

TIP
While you are stretching your legs on your walking tour, stop at the corner of 8th and College to warm your hands (or buns) at the built-in brick fireplace. Hungry walkers can even swing in to Kilwin's Chocolates and grab a sweet treat.

SUPPORT A LOCAL FAMILY BUSINESS
AT APOTHECARY GIFT SHOP

Apothecary Gift Shop, on the corner of River and 8th, is on the list of family-run businesses you won't want to miss.

The shop was established in the late 1800s as Model Drug Store and served the community faithfully for many years. In 1961, the Ditch family purchased the drug store and have spent the years since modernizing and making it into the gift shop that has become a cherished part of the Holland Community. The best part? Apothecary Gift Shop gives back to the community in countless ways, like donating items to the Power H shop at Holland Public School, where families can obtain needed items for free.

Apothecary is the perfect place to pick up a Michigan-themed trinket or treat, a unique toy, a puzzle, a game, or even something for the bath. Like Vera Bradley? Find it here, along with Pandora items and a room full of unique jewelry.

35 W 8th St., 616-392-4707
apothecarygiftshop.com

PURCHASE A FAIR TRADE GIFT
AT THE BRIDGE

In a world where you can be anything, be kind. One way to do so is to share our wealth with those around the world who don't have the same opportunities we have. The Bridge Fair Trade Gifts & Cards store is the perfect example. Your purchase at the Bridge supports communities around the world.

The Bridge is an outreach of Holland's Western Theological Seminary (WTS), which partners with artisans worldwide to offer goods right here in Holland at fair market prices!

People who love global travel will love the Bridge, which brings the globe home to our downtown. My favorite item is undoubtedly the variety of nativity sets. Look around and you will find examples of artisan work from countries such as Guatemala, Mexico, and Kenya. Scarves, jewelry, kitchen items, and home decor are all available and make excellent gifts or additions to your home collection.

18 W 8th St., 616-392-3977
thebridgefairtrade.com

SHRINK YOUR FAMILY FOOTPRINT WHEN SHOPPING
AT ECOBUNS BABY & CO.

In today's consumer-obsessed, disposable-everything world, we need more stores like Ecobuns, which sells environmentally responsible products and heirloom-quality toys meant for a lifetime of cherishing.

The mother–daughter team of Vicki and Marissa have a passion for serving their community and customers and are often in the store and ready to show you their newest product! Besides the large variety of durable and imaginative toys, Ecobuns also carries eco-friendly and natural baby products, feeding accessories, and clothing items.

Keep an eye on the Ecobuns's social media accounts to stay abreast of in-store activities for parents and kids. This store is always hopping! The one danger of shopping here for toys is that you'll have to carefully choose what to buy, because it will likely become a part of your collection for generations!

11975 E Lakewood Blvd., #6, 616-395-5555
ecobuns.com

TIP

Ecobuns works very hard to keep their inventory battery-free. All the toys in the store are powered by pure imagination!

KNIT AN HEIRLOOM
AT GARENHUIS YARN STUDIO

Garenhuis is Dutch for "yarn house" and is the perfect place to cozy up with your favorite ball of yarn and knit yourself a treasure. Garenhuis carries a generous selection of yarns and blends in cotton, silk, wool, camel, and even yak hair, along with more notions than you could ask for! When you visit Garenhuis, you're visiting family, so come in any time to ask questions or work on your latest project. Don't be surprised if you leave with more than a fun, new project after a visit. You may walk away with a new friend, too.

If you are new to yarn arts and want to learn or improve your skillset, sign up for a class. With a hands-on class at Garenhuis, you'll learn by doing. Before you know it, you'll be cuddled up with your own cozy, hand-knitted treasure and planning your next one!

27 W 9th St., #110, 616-294-3492
garenhuis.com

GET ALL YOUR QUESTIONS ANSWERED
AT THE HOLLAND AREA VISITORS BUREAU

By now, you must think there's nothing left to do in Holland that we haven't explored. But you would be incorrect. Holland, Michigan, has more wonderful restaurants, shops, beaches, outdoor adventures, and cultural and entertainment experiences than you could imagine.

I wish I could talk about everything here in town, but since my time and space are limited, I will leave the rest up to the fantastic staff at the Holland Area Visitor's Bureau. As you're cruising down 8th Street, stop in where you see the giant wooden shoes in front of the door. The experts there can answer all of your questions. Be sure and take your photo while standing in those oversized shoes while you're there! A visit to Holland isn't complete without a picture in a giant pair of wooden shoes!

78 E 8th St., 616-394-0000
holland.org

FEEL GOOD
AT GEZELLIG

The first thing you'll notice when you enter Gezellig in downtown Holland is the joyful greeting. No matter how often you stop in, the folks at Gezellig are happy to see you! This darling shop's name pays tribute to Holland's Dutch heritage. Gezellig is the Dutch word that translates roughly to "feels good." You may hear other translations such as comfortable, cozy, welcoming, or similar, but that's because Gezellig doesn't have a perfect translation. Just like the store, it is unique, memorable, and cherished!

Owners Tony and Melissa are great supporters of the local arts, and the items in their store reflect this. You'll find a great variety of items for sale, from greeting cards to home goods, all created by locals. When you shop at Gezellig, you'll be supporting not only this shop but also our local artists!

188 S River Ave., 616-928-2625
gezellighome.net

STEP UP YOUR FASHION STYLE
AT JEAN MARIE'S

Jean Marie's offers the hottest fashion finds in sizes S to 3XL, perfect for just about every shape and size! Proud graduates of Holland's own Hope College, the husband/wife team who owns Jean Marie's are active participants in the local community. Jean Marie's hosts multiple events throughout the year, including back-to-school parties, fashion shows, and special shopping days. They even have an app for those who want to shop from afar! Customer service is the word at Jean Marie's, and don't be surprised if one of their fantastic staff offers you a delightful beverage while you shop.

And if fashion isn't your thing, stop at the downtown location to pick up a Yeti product or something from their finely curated selection of items for your home. Come to one of Jean Marie's two Holland locations if you're looking for fashion, fun, or downhome, friendly service.

486 Chicago Dr., 616-796-8844
jeanmaries.com

WATCH TIME TICK BY
AT THE HOLLAND CLOCK COMPANY

The tick-tock sound of the running clocks is so soothing when you enter the Holland Clock Company. The next best thing is being in the shop at the hour when you can hear all of the hundreds of clocks chiming their notice.

But the sounds of these unique and individual clocks are only part of the fun. Pay attention to the tiny details on each of these treasures and you'll have difficulty finding a reason to leave. Holland Clock Company has been Holland's retailer of German Black Forest Cuckoo Clocks, German Novelty clocks, and Black Forest Miniature Clocks since 2010.

In its lifetime, this unique shop has moved twice around Holland, each time growing in size to extend its product line. So, if a clock isn't for you, come in and check out the German beer steins, smokers, nutcrackers, Christmas pyramids, and wooden ornaments, too!

39 E 8th St., 616-298-2612
hollandclockcompany.com

BENEFIT HOLLAND AND THE WORLD
BY SHOPPING AT B2 OUTLET STORES

B2 Outlet Stores are more than just a place to get a great bargain. B2, the shortened name that originated as "Bid-2-Benefit-Youth," has become a thriving merchant in Holland, selling everything from food to electronics, toys, and games, clothing, and home and patio goods.

B2 purchases and resells liquidated goods. Founders and father/son team Duane and Matt began the business in 2014. Since then, the company has thrived in our Holland community and now includes 20 other locations around West Michigan. But what makes this business special is the focus on ministry, both here in Holland and worldwide. B2 selects a mission of the month, and since 2014 they have given over a million dollars to local and global causes.

When you make a purchase at B2, you can feel confident that your purchase contributes to our local community and missions worldwide.

710 Chicago Dr., #270, 616-772-1967
b2outlets.com

MAKE A STOP
ON THE ANTIQUE TRAIL
AT NOT SO SHABBY MARKETPLACE

Antiques are as much a part of the American experience as apple pie and baseball. The Not So Shabby Marketplace features over 70 booths fully stocked with unique and compelling antique items. This one-of-a-kind shop is one of the best places in Holland to add to your antique collection.

Need a genuine silver spoon? A particular wall hanging? Want to add to your vintage Coca-Cola collection? Chances are high you'll find those items and many, many more. But what's best about Not So Shabby is that new items arrive daily. And in addition to the antiques there are handcrafted items and many refurbished household pieces that would make a perfect addition to your home or man cave.

Each booth has its unique style, and traveling down the aisles is akin to walking through 70 individual stores in one! The Not So Shabby Marketplace is a member of antiquetrail.com.

2975 W Shore Dr., 616-796-6980
notsoshabbyholland.com

ACTIVATE YOUR SENSES
AT GARSNETT BEACON CANDLE CO.

Holland's downtown landscape is always changing, growing, and expanding for new dreamers and doers. The Garsnett Beacon Candle Co. owners, Chad and Sebastian Garsnett, brought their dreams to life when they opened their first brick-and-mortar store in downtown Holland in 2022. Now they are doing what they love and sharing their vision by offering a unique hands-on experience unlike any other in Holland.

They have taken their dream one step further by contributing to many nonprofits in the community that champion diversity, equity, and inclusion.

Schedule a time with Garsnett Beacon Candle Co. to celebrate a special event in your scent-mixing, candle-making experience. Sniff a few or all 80 available fragrances, select a vessel, blend the ones you love, and pour it all into your custom candle to take home.

210 S River Ave., 616-287-3444
garsnettbeacon.com

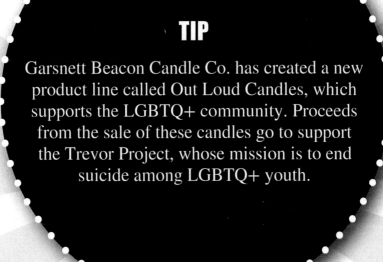

TIP

Garsnett Beacon Candle Co. has created a new product line called Out Loud Candles, which supports the LGBTQ+ community. Proceeds from the sale of these candles go to support the Trevor Project, whose mission is to end suicide among LGBTQ+ youth.

SUGGESTED
ITINERARIES

HISTORY BUFFS

Take a Walk down Memory Lane at the Holland Museum, 88

Take Home a Piece of Holland's History from the Holland Bowl Mill, 117

Learn about Life before City Water at the Pump House Museum
and Learning Center, 96

Stand in the Shoes of Holland's Early Residents at the Cappon House
& Settler's Museum, 89

Muster Up Your Troops at the VanRaalte Farm Civil War Muster, 95

Learn the Secrets of Holland with Holland Tasting Tours, 6

Take Time for History (and a Selfie) at the Clock Tower, 93

Soak In a Historical Sleep at the Centennial Inn Bed & Breakfast, 90

Relive a Historical Shootout at the Warm Friend, 94

FREEBIES

Feel the Freedom at the Independence Day Fireworks Celebration, 40

Walk Safely on Snowmelt Sidewalks, 119

Get All Your Questions Answered at the Holland Area Visitors Bureau, 125

Party Hearty at the Annual LAUP Fiesta, 46

Pack a Picnic and Practice Your Dance Moves at Kollen Park's Summer
Concert Series, 34

Celebrate a World of Music at the International Festival of Holland, 51

Find Your Inner Artist by Painting and Hiding Rocks, 86

Take In the Local Talent with the Summer Street Performer Series, 48

Learn about Life before City Water at the Pump House Museum
and Learning Center, 96

• •

A DAY ON THE WATER

Walk through a Dune at Tunnel Park, 58

Make a Splash at the Holland Aquatic Center, 74

Say Goodnight to the Sun at Holland State Park Beach, 60

Spend a Day on the Lake with Holland Water Sports, 57

Have a Hands-On Sailing Experience with Deep Lake Ventures Sailboat Charters, 72

Paddle Your Heart Out with Tulip City Paddle Tours, 63

Get Your Fill of Fish at Boatwerks Waterfront Restaurant, 25

Give Your Pedometer a Workout at Holland State Park Pier, 59

Catch Tonight's Dinner with a Sport Fishing Charter, 70

FOR THE TULIP LOVER

Say Hello to Dutch St. Nicholas at Magic at the Mill, 100

Enjoy the World's Biggest Tulip Festival at the Annual Tulip Time Festival, 104

Klomp Your Way through Dutch Culture at Nelis' Dutch Village, 102

Tiptoe through the Tulips at Veldheer Tulip Gardens, 98

Get inside a Real Working Windmill at Windmill Island Garden, 101

DATE NIGHT

Say Hello to Fresh Food and Friendly Service at Waverly Stone Gastropub, 15

Cheer On the Home Team with a Hope College Athletics Event, 68

Tickle Your Tongue with a Premium Crafted Spirit at Coppercraft Distillery, 22

Say Goodnight to the Sun at Holland State Park Beach, 60

Taste the Finer Things in Life at Butch's Dry Dock, 26

Listen for the Whinny at Crazy Horse Steakhouse, 9

Feel the History of Holland at Park Theater, 38

Get Your Fill of Fish at Boatwerks Waterfront Restaurant, 25

Step into the Future at Zero Latency Holland, 50

Let the Music Take You Away at Holland Symphony Orchestra, 53

• •

CHRISTMAS

Say Hello to Dutch St. Nicholas at Magic at the Mill, 100

Attend an Event at Holland Civic Center Place, 42

Wave Hello to Santa at the Parade of Lights, 108

CRAFT LOVERS

Activate Your Senses at Garsnett Beacon Candle Co., 132

Find Your Inner Artist by Painting and Hiding Rocks, 86

Create a Keepsake at Paint a Pot Studio, 106

Surround Yourself with Artistry at the Holland Area Arts Council, 85

Color Your Way to Fun at Carolyn Stich Studio & Gift Shop, 107

Knit an Heirloom at Garenhuis Yarn Studio, 124

MUSIC LOVERS

Feel the History of Holland at Park Theater, 38

Let the Music Take You Away at Holland Symphony Orchestra, 53

Party Hearty at the Annual LAUP Fiesta, 46

Pack a Picnic and Practice Your Dance Moves at Kollen Park's Summer Concert Series, 34

Celebrate a World of Music at the International Festival of Holland, 51

COFFEE LOVERS

Belly Up to a Delicious Brew at the 205 Coffee Bar, 18

Sip a Cider and Taste a Pie at Crane's in the City, 29

Practice Your Pronunciation at Lemonjello's, 20

Indulge in a Bacon-Flavored Donut at DeBoer Bakkerij
and Dutch Brothers Restaurant, 10

SPORTSMAN

Shoosh through Blankets of Snow at Pigeon Creek Park, 76

Paddle Your Heart Out with Tulip City Paddle Tours, 63

Catch Tonight's Dinner with a Sport Fishing Charter, 70

Spend a Day on the Lake with Holland Water Sports, 57

Cheer On the Home Team with a Hope College Athletics Event, 68

Have a Hands-On Sailing Experience with Deep Lake Ventures Sailboat Charters, 72

Rent an E-Bike at Velo City Cycles, 78

Strap on a Pair of Ice Skates at Griff's Icehouse West, 62

UNIQUE SHOPPING

Step Up Your Fashion Style at Jean Marie's, 127

Make a Stop on the Antique Trail at Not So Shabby Marketplace, 130

Take Home a Piece of Holland's History from the Holland Bowl Mill, 117

Watch Time Tick By at the Holland Clock Company, 128

Become a Part of the Family at Cento Anni Custom Woodworking, 118

Purchase a Fair Trade Gift at the Bridge, 121

Tiptoe through the Tulips at Veldheer Tulip Gardens, 98

Benefit Holland and the World by Shopping at B2 Outlet Stores, 129

Color Your Way to Fun at Carolyn Stich Studio & Gift Shop, 107

Feel Good at Gezellig, 126

Shrink Your Family Footprint when Shopping at Ecobuns Baby & Co., 122

• •

ACTIVITIES
BY SEASON

SPRING

Lower Your Blood Pressure at Window on the Waterfront, 80

Enjoy the World's Biggest Tulip Festival at the Annual Tulip Time Festival, 104

Discover the Outdoors at the Outdoor Discovery Center, 65

Get inside a Real Working Windmill at Windmill Island Garden, 101

Rent an E-Bike at Velo City Cycles, 78

Find Your Inner Artist by Painting and Hiding Rocks, 86

Get the Best View of Lake Michigan on Mt. Pisgah, 61

Tiptoe through the Tulips at Veldheer Tulip Gardens, 98

Klomp Your Way through Dutch Culture at Nelis' Dutch Village, 102

SUMMER

Take In the Local Talent with the Summer Street Performer Series, 48

Taste a Tommy Turtle at Captain Sundae, 8

Pack a Picnic and Practice Your Dance Moves at Kollen Park's Summer Concert Series, 34

Learn about Life before City Water at the Pump House Museum and Learning Center, 96

Thrill Your Inner Thespian at Hope College Repertory Theatre, 36

Party Hearty at the Annual LAUP Fiesta, 46

Feel the Freedom at the Independence Day Fireworks Celebration, 40

Reap a Local Harvest at the Holland Farmers Market, 113

Taste Blueberry-Flavored Everything at Bowerman's Blueberries, 2

Get Educated about Agriculture at the Ottawa County Fair, 47

Cruise Past Big Red on the *Holland Princess*, 109

• •

FALL

Sip a Cider and Taste a Pie at Crane's in the City, 29

Nurture Nature at DeGraaf Nature Center, 64

Muster Up Your Troops at the VanRaalte Farm Civil War Muster, 95

Rent an E-Bike at Velo City Cycles, 78

Celebrate a World of Music at the International Festival of Holland, 51

Learn the Secrets of Holland with Holland Tasting Tours, 6

Pet a Pig or a Pony at Fellinlove Farm, 56

Get the Best View of Lake Michigan on Mt. Pisgah, 61

Cheer On the Home Team with a Hope College Athletics Event, 68

WINTER

Feel the History of Holland at Park Theater, 38

Wave Hello to Santa at the Parade of Lights, 108

Increase Artistic Awareness at Knickerbocker Theatre, 39

Strap on a Pair of Ice Skates at Griff's Icehouse West, 62

Cheer On the Home Team with a Hope College Athletics Event, 68

Make a Splash at the Holland Aquatic Center, 74

Create a Keepsake at Paint a Pot Studio, 106

Soak Up the Local Talent at Holland Community Theatre, 35

Embrace Your Inner Child at BAM! Entertainment Center, 67

Take a Walk down Memory Lane at the Holland Museum, 88

Shoosh through Blankets of Snow at Pigeon Creek Park, 76

Say Hello to Dutch St. Nicholas at Magic at the Mill, 100

• •

INDEX

205 Coffee Bar, 18–19

AMC Holland 8, 45

Antique Trail, 130–131

Antiques, 13, 130–131

Apothecary Gift Shop, 120

B2 Outlet Stores, 129

Bachelor One, 71

Baja Grill, 31

BAM! Entertainment Center, 67

Bambu Holland, 21

Beachside Bike Rental (in Oak Grove Campground), 79

Beau H2O Excursions, 71

Bending Limits Sportfishing Charters, 71

Biscuit Café, The, 24

Black Pearl Sportfishing, 71

Boatwerks Waterfront Restaurant, 25, 40

Bowerman's Blueberries, 2–3

Bowling, 67

Bridge, The, 121

Butch's Dry Dock, 26

Cappon House & Settler's Museum, 88, 89

Captain Sundae, 8

Carolyn Stich Studio & Gift Shop, 107

Carpe Latte, 21

Centennial Inn Bed & Breakfast, 89

Centennial Park, 87, 88, 91, 92

Cento Anni Custom Woodworking, 118

Clock Tower, 93

Coffee shops, 20–21

CoHooker Charter, 71

Coppercraft Distillery, 22

Crane's in the City, 29

Crazy Horse Steakhouse, 9

Cross Country Cycle, 79

Curragh, The, 7

DeBoer Bakkerij and Dutch Brothers Restaurant, 10–11

Deep Lake Ventures Sailboat Charter, 72

Deep V Sportfishing Charters, 71

DeGraaf Nature Center, 64

Don Miguel, 31

Downtown Antiques & Home Furnishings, 131

Dutch food, 104

Dutch Village, 84, 102–103

Ecobuns Baby & Co., 122–123

El Huarache, 31

Eldean's Shipyard Marina, 70, 72

Fat Burrito, 31

Fellinlove Farm, 56

Ferris Coffee, 21

Fillmore Discovery Park, 77

Fricano's Too, 28

Fustini's Oil & Vinegar, 116

Garenhuis Yarn Studio, 124

Garsnett Beacon Candle Co., 132–133

Gezellig, 126

Good Earth Café, 21

Goog's Pub & Grub, 17
GQT Holland 7, 45
Griff's Icehouse West, 62
Harvest Antiques, Collectibles and
    Home Décor, 131
Herrick District Library, 52, 87
Holland Aquatic Center, 74
Holland Area Arts Council, 85
Holland Bowl Mill, 117
Holland Civic Center, 42–43, 46, 51,
    104, 108, 113
Holland Clock Company, 128
Holland Community Theatre, 35
Holland Farmers Market, 42, 113
Holland Museum, 88, 89
Holland Oz Exhibit, 87
Holland Princess, 109
Holland State Park Beach, 8, 60
Holland State Park Pier, 59
Holland Symphony Orchestra, 53
Holland Tasting Tours, 6
Holland Visitor Center, 81
Holland Water Sports, 57
Hope College Athletics, 68
Hope College Repertory Theatre, 36
Huyser Farm Park, 77
Ice cream, 8, 14, 60, 61, 115
Independence Day Fireworks
    Celebration, 40
J.D. Charters, 71
Jean Marie's, 127
JJ Sportfishing Charters, 71
Joe2Go LLC, 21
KIN Coffee and Craft House, 21
Knickerbocker Theatre, 39, 45

Kollen Park, 34, 40
Kollen Park's Summer Concert Series,
    34
Kruizenga Art Museum, 105
LAUP Fiesta, 42, 46
Lemonjello's, 20
Lost City, The, 66
Magic at the Mill, 100
Margaritas, 30
Mi Favorita Grocery, 31
Mt. Pisgah, 61
N' Pursuit Charters LLC, 71
Nancy Anne Sailing, 73
New Holland Brewing Company, 16, 38
Nob Hill Again, 131
Not So Shabby Marketplace, 130
Ottawa County Fair, 47
Outdoor Discovery Center, 65, 77
Paint a Pot Studio, 106
Paint and hide rocks, 86
Parade of Lights, 108
Park Theater, 38
Peachwave, 14
Peanut Store, 115
Pigeon Creek Park, 76
Powderhorn Sportfishing Charters, 71
Public Art around Holland, 92
Pump House Museum and Learning
    Center, 96–97
Radventures, 79
Reader's World, 114
Reel Talk Sportfishing Charters, 71
Riley Trails Park, 77
Russ' Restaurant, 4–5, 6

• •

Sailing Mac Charters, 73
Saugatuck Dunes State Park, 77
Sculptures, 87, 92, 105
Seedlings Boutique, 112, 131
Simpatico Coffee Joint, 21
Skiles Tavern, 27
Snowmelt sidewalks, 23, 119
Sperry's Moviehouse, 44
Sport Fishing Charters, 70–71
SuFISHient Charters, 71
Summer Street Performer Series, 48
Supermarket Rosie, 31
Taco Fiesta, 31
Tacos El Cuñado, 31
Taqueria Arandas, 31
Taqueria Vallarta, 31
Teerman Lofts, 84
Tienda Azteca, 31
Tulip City Paddle Tours, 63
Tulip Time Festival, 42–43, 47, 90–91, 104, 107, 109

Tunnel Park, 58
Uncle Jibs Ski & Kayak Shop, 77
Unsalted Outfitters, 71
VanBuren Park Dune Trails, 77
VanRaalte Farm Civil War Muster, 95
VanRaalte Farm Park, 77, 95
Veldheer Tulip Gardens, 98
Velo City Cycles, 78
Video games, 66
Warm Friend, the, 94
Waverly Stone Gastropub, 15
Way Cup Café, 21
West Michigan Bike and Fitness, 79
Windmill Island, 63, 100, 101
Windmill Restaurant, The, 23
Window on the Waterfront, 80
Wooden Shoe Antique Mall, 13, 131
Wooden Shoe Restaurant, 12–13
Wooden shoes, 98, 104, 117, 125
Yacht Basin Marina, 70, 72–73
Zero Latency, 50